Eclipse of God

MARTIN BUBER

ECLIPSE OF GOD

Studies in the Relation Between Religion and Philosophy

with introduction by

Robert M. Seltzer
Jewish Social Studies
Hunter College

HUMANITIES PRESS INTERNATIONAL, INC.
Atlantic Highlands, NJ

This edition first published with a new introduction, 1988,
in the United States of America by
HUMANITIES PRESS INTERNATIONAL, INC.,
Atlantic Highlands, NJ 07716

**LIBRARY OF CONGRESS
CATALOGING-IN-PUBLICATION DATA**

Buber, Martin, 1878–1965.
  Eclipse of God.

  Translation of: Gottesfinsternis.
  Includes bibliographies and index.
  1. Religion—Philosophy.   2. Philosophy and religion.
I. Title.
BL51.B8213   1988   200'.1   87–19594
ISBN 0–391–03533–9 (pbk.)

Printed in the United States of America
10 9   8   7   6

Contents

Foreword

THIS BOOK ARISES OUT OF LECTURES WHICH I GAVE AT SEVERAL American universities (Yale, Princeton, Columbia, Chicago and others) in the months of November and December, 1951. I have placed first, as an appropriate prelude, the "Report on Two Talks" which I wrote in 1932, and I have also included the essay "The Love of God and the Idea of Deity," written in 1943. In the section "Religion and Philosophy" I have used some passages from the address on this subject with which I opened the 1929 session of the Schopenhauer Society at Frankfurt a. M., devoted to this theme.

"Report on Two Talks," "Religion and Philosophy," "Religion and Modern Thinking," "On the Suspension of the Ethical," "God and the Spirit of Man" and the supplement "Reply to C. G. Jung" were translated by Maurice S. Friedman. "Religion and Ethics" was translated by Eugene Kamenka and Maurice S. Friedman. "Religion and Reality" was translated by Norbert Guterman. "The Love of God and the Idea of Deity" was translated by I. M. Lask, and is reprinted from my book entitled *Israel and the World: Essays in a Time of Crisis*, copyright, 1948; a Shocken Book, Farrar, Straus and Young, Inc., publishers, and reprinted with their permission.

MARTIN BUBER

Introduction

MARTIN Buber's upbringing and education embraced the contrasting worlds of East European Judaism and the modern secular West. Born in Vienna in 1878, Buber spent his childhood in his grandfather's home in Galicia, a province of the Austro-Hungarian empire populated largely by Poles, Ukrainians, and Jews, including many traditionally observant religious Jews. Buber's grandfather was a distinguished historian of midrash, a branch of ancient rabbinic literature. In Lvov, where his grandfather lived, young Buber became acquainted with Hasidism, the Jewish pietistic movement about which he was later to write so extensively, but Buber's own schooling was thoroughly modern. At universities in Vienna, Leipzig, Zurich, and Berlin he studied philosophy and art history, and his taste and intellectual style were shaped by sophisticated Central European literature and thought of the turn of the twentieth century.

While still a student Buber became an ardent Zionist, attaching himself to the spiritual or cultural Zionism that had formed around the Hebrew essayist Ahad Ha-Am (the pen name of the Asher Ginzberg). Critical of Theodor Herzl's preoccupation with political aims and diplomatic tactics, Ahad Ha-Am and his disciples saw as the supreme task of Zionism the rebirth of the Jewish tradition to full creative vitality. In contrast to what they considered a truncated, home-and-synagogue-centered existence to which Judaism had been confined in Western countries since the end of the eighteenth century, return to Zion provided a physical setting for cultural rebirth through restoration of social condi-

tions permitting full Jewish communal life in the land of
Israel. Jewish renewal was to be a constant concern of
Buber's. From 1916 to 1928 he edited the literary journal *Der
Jude* (The Jew), among whose contributors were some of the
most eminent twentieth-century European writers and think-
ers seeking, like Buber, to recover and express their roots in
Jewish civilization in a modern, yet authentic manner.

In the years before World War I Buber began to produce a
steady stream of books, mostly in German, that earned him a
reputation as one of the most brilliant and controversial
Jewish thinkers of the twentieth century. His first, rather
romantic writings on mysticism include free translations of
legends about eighteenth-century Hasidic rabbis. Other early
essays called for a new "Hebrew humanism" based on biblical insights. Buber's social thought indicated a strong sym-
pathy to utopian and ethical socialism, rather than to the
"scientific" Marxist socialism which stressed impersonal historical forces and centralized control. Buber's Zionism fa-
vored small-scale cooperative communities, exemplified by
the *kibbutsim* established by the Zionist movement in the
land of Israel just before World War I.

In 1922 Buber published *I and Ti   ʻ*, the seminal presenta-
tion of the philosophy of dialogue tɪ   had come to dominate
his thinking. From the mid-1920s he taught Jewish thought at
the University of Frankfurt-on-Main and collaborated with
the German-Jewish theologian Franz Rosenzweig on a new
translation of the Hebrew Bible into German. The Buber-
Rosenzweig translation deliberately sought to convey the
directness and living force of the ancient biblical word.
Among Buber's most stimulating books were studies, in-
formed by his dialogical philosophy, of early Israelite religion and the faith of the biblical prophets.

In 1933, when Germany fell under Nazi rule and the Jews were stripped of political and civil rights, Buber became director of adult education for German Jewry. In the face of increasing Nazi persecution, he sought to encourage Jewish self-discovery and spiritual revival. But transformation of Germany into a totalitarian, racial state dashed hopes for even a limited Jewish presence there. In 1938 Buber settled in Jerusalem as professor of social philosophy at the Hebrew University. In Palestine he became active in the Ihud group devoted to Arab-Jewish understanding with the goal in mind of a joint Arab-Jewish commonwealth (it foundered on the lack of significant Arab participation). Besides teaching and writing on Jewish and philosophical subjects and involvement in a wide range of cultural and educational undertakings in Israel, after World War II Buber lectured in Europe and the United States, where his philosophy of dialogue attracted attention from psychologists, educators, Christian theologians, and rabbis. (Most of the material in *Eclipse of God* originated in a series of lectures he delivered at American universities in 1951.) Buber died in Jerusalem in 1965.

The gist of Buber's writings is the centrality of the relationship between two who speak and listen to each other, a relationship which coincides with Buber's interpretation of the concept of revelation, his understanding of the nature of human existence, and his conception of the limits of rationalist philosophy.

For Buber, nothing—no possible insight, report, or knowledge at all—can substitute for confronting an other directly and immediately. Experiences, events, relations can be described and analyzed, but description, no matter how vivid, and analysis, no matter how acute, cannot serve as alternatives for responsiveness, "here and now," between two

subjects "over against each other." The two subjects in this
relation Buber calls by the pronouns "I" and "Thou" (most
appropriate in languages whose grammars distinguish the
second-person-singular with strong overtones of intimacy
from the more impersonal second-person-plural). The Thou
that I encounter is not a mere object, it is a subject in its own
right that confirms the I in recognizing and addressing it. The
Thou, in turn, is recognized and addressed by the I, so that
the I and the Thou, as they directly respond to each other,
are united in a symmetrical bond that maintains their indivi-
dualities but brings them into living relation with each other.
By way of contrast, in the I-It mode the I observes or makes
use of the other (according to Buber, this "It" can be a thing
or a person). Because no persons exist independently of their
relationships, the I takes on a different character in the two
primary modes: in the I-It the I judges and observes in the
context of an established scheme of things, whereas in the
I-Thou the I risks his or her security by listening as well as
speaking, ready to receive something new and to respond in
a new manner.

Fundamental to Buber, therefore, is a concept of being
which involves mutuality, personhood, spontaneity, present-
ness. We necessarily move back and forth between I-Thou
and I-It. Buber insists that he does not disparage the value of
I-It relations, which are required for the practical skills and
scientific achievements of human life. But, he claims, in
modern times the sheer quantity of I-It threatens to overwhelm the openness that is a condition of realizing personal
and social good. Domination by I-It is particularly fatal in
matters of the spirit because, for Buber, the basis of authentic religious existence is the revelatory encounter of the
whole human being and the unique other that Buber calls the
eternal Thou.

In Buber's philosophy, God is the eternal Thou, the ground of all specific Thous. God addresses and is addressed by the I in the full range of unique situations and occurrences of everyday life, as well as in moments of extraordinary power and destiny that are the formative moments of traditional religions. With some reluctance, perhaps, Buber accepts as the root of belief in God in traditional religions, a series of historic encounters with the eternal Thou (*Eclipse of God*, pp. 17–18).

Why Buber's reluctance? Because for him God is the Thou that can never become It. As pure Thouness, God is not objectifiable. Words serve only as mute gestures pointing to the irreducible, ineffable dimension where God subsists. God cannot be a metaphysical concept, a doctrinal term, a liturgical allusion. Buber claims to have become disenchanted with much mysticism when he understood that God is not found by fleeing the world to private moments of mystical union; God is met in the social world with its concrete social demands and ethical duties. For Buber all doctrines, commandments, and even narratives of revelation, without exception, fall in the realm of I-It. Revelation as the relation of an I to the eternal Thou is always spontaneous, it always occurs only in the present, and it occurs if one is in a state of readiness to receive it.

Can the experience of revelation ever provide content, in addition to memory of ineffable confirmation? In much of Buber's writings it would seem that revelation leaves one charged with a sense of meaning but cannot give rise to any specific insight or any imperative. When criticized that his approach cut out the ground from under the authority of sacred law or ritual, Buber agreed. He was, however, intensely interested in the Jewish record of revelatory relationships between the community and the eternal Thou. For

Buber, the Bible recounts the responses of ancient Israel to the eternal Thou as the covenantal community came to understand itself as holy nation. We have noted that biblical revelation is for Buber identical in principle with revelations available to us in our everyday lives. It is therefore possible for moderns to appropriate the experience that lies behind the biblical record, as well as the experience that lies behind other moments of genuine religious spontaneity in the past. In this regard, particularly appealing to Buber were the communities formed around the great Hasidic masters in Eastern Europe during the late eighteenth century. The Hasidic teaching that God was to be found in all things, Buber interpreted as indicating that the Hasidic masters taught that the here-and-now is to be hallowed rather than escaped from, and that God is to be worshipped in all dimensions of life, not only in acts of formal worship.

To summarize: in Buber's view, at the heart of all genuine religiosity (which may or may not take place in religious circumstances as conventionally understood) is the opening up of everyday reality to dialogic relations with an eternal, everpresent, absolute Thou. But the conditions of modern life and the teachings of many scholars have created an ambience where many are increasingly blind to this reality. This condition Buber called the "eclipse of God." Even religion and philosophy live in the shadow of this eclipse.

We have seen that for Buber the most urgent task is to rescue the primacy of the mutual encounter of one person with another. No mere description, however profound or vivacious, can take the place of actual meeting. In *Eclipse of God* Buber is concerned with the extent to which modern thought has become indifferent or even hostile to the immediacy of human contact with the divine Thou. *Eclipse of God* is a collection of essays in which Buber contrasts his dialogic approach with some of the most important intellectual currents of twentieth-century continental Europe, including neo-Kantianism, existentialism, and psychoanalysis.

From the German-Jewish tradition, Buber singles out Hermann Cohen, a thoughtful exponent of Jewish religious liberalism and one of the most eminent interpreters of Kant and spokesman for the neo-Kantian movement in late nineteenth-century Germany. In Cohen's Jewish writings, the God of ethical monotheism is the pivotal notion within a comprehensive grid of philosophically valid concepts through which reality is to be grasped. The God-idea guarantees the progressive realization of man's ethical task in history that is the basis of Judaism's hopeful vision of human destiny. Buber was himself not a little indebted to Cohen, especially to Cohen's notion of "correlation" as characterizing the reciprocal relation between God and man. But in the essay entitled "The Love of God and the Idea of Deity," Buber criticizes Cohen's conception that one can love God (or anyone) *only* as an ideal. For Buber, love is the relationship that subsists between two real persons, prior to any idealizing by one of another. According to Buber, the pure idea of God in a system of thought such as Cohen's, albeit noble and rational, is still a mere "image of images" of the imageless God whom man loves as an actuality. A critic could ask, however, whether Buber is too easy on himself by indicating that he has demolished the philosophical idealism of Cohen merely by insisting that his own conceptual system points to reality as it actually is. Does not Buber's dichotomy of I-It and I-Thou constitute a metaphysical assertion subject to logical testing and requiring comprehensive rational defense? It would seem that Buber's notion of an eternal Thou as an underlying and integrating Thouness, is quite as much a philosophical construction as Cohen's idealistic God.

"Religion and Ethics" is Buber's most extended historical discussion, in *Eclipse of God*, of the attempt to bind the distinction between good and evil to absolute reality. Buber is especially concerned about the "art of mistrust" that "seeks to unmask the spiritual world as a system of deceptions and self-deceptions, of 'ideologies' and 'sublimations.'" In this regard, a nineteenth-century figure of considerable notoriety was Ludwig Feuerbach, who "unmasked" God and religion as projections of human needs. Feuerbach was a major influence on Karl Marx, who subsumed all religious systems under the notion of a superstructure erected by human economic needs and relations in order to justify class interests. For Marx, all moral, political, philosophical, and theological ideas were epiphenomenal manifestations of the historical process, not glimpses of an absolute. In his essay Buber concentrates on yet another major nineteenth-century figure, Friedrich Nietzsche. Buber takes special issue with Nietzsche's conception of the will-to-power as the basis of the life of the spirit. He accepts Nietzsche's diagnosis that "nihilism" is the direct consequence of the radical doubt and philosophical mistrust characteristic of the modern mentality. For Nietzsche, this radical doubt leads to the eventual loss of value even on the part of the traditionally highest values. What is the way out of the impasse? Buber rejects Nietzsche's prophecy that a new, completely free heroic type, a super-man, will emerge to create novel life-affirming values for humankind. Nietzsche had epitomized the modern situation as the "death of God": the absolute postulated by religion can no longer serve as ground for value. For Buber, Nietzsche's own "biological" scale of values—substituting an ethics of strong versus weak for one of good versus evil—was no scale of value at all, and therefore no solution to the dilemma of twentieth-century civilization.

Another nineteenth-century thinker who exerted a considerable influence on Buber was the Danish theologian Sören Kierkegaard. In "On the Suspension of the Ethical," Buber discusses Kierkegaard's *Fear and Trembling*, which uses the story of Abraham's binding of Isaac in Genesis 22 as a springboard for suggesting that a moral duty can at times be suspended or superseded by higher obedience to God. Buber asks how one knows he is being addressed by God when he feels asked to sacrifice that which is dearest to him. Was it so self-evident that the voice Abraham heard (or anyone can hear) was really God's voice? In our age—Buber is alluding to Nazi Germany and the Soviet Union under Stalin—honest men lie and torture and kill for Moloch, a false absolute; they believe quite sincerely that lying and torturing and killing will prepare the way for social justice and world peace. In the end, Buber rejects Kierkegaard's "teleological suspension of the ethical": Genesis 22 has to be complemented with Micah 6:8, which teaches that the true sacrifice that God demands is righteousness, mercy, and humility.

Against the liberal religion exemplified by Hermann Cohen, Buber had held that religion cannot be reduced to the ethical; against the neo-orthodox religion adumbrated by Kierkegaard, Buber holds that the ethical can never be suspended. We can ask if Buber does not weaken his own position by his criticism of Kierkegaard. Certainly Buber owes us a more extended answer to how a revelatory voice can be identified as the voice of a God of goodness. Does not Buber's notion of the non-objectifiable character of revelation render difficult, if not impossible, the discernment of a divine standard by which human ethical conduct can be measured, and call into question the very insight that Micah 6:8 and the Jewish tradition take as a supreme commandment?

The unifying theme of *Eclipse of God* is that the radical subjectivism of modern thought has blocked access to the transcendent, resulting in a spiritual blindness to the living presence of God. The I-It has usurped, practically uncontested, mastery and rule of contemporary technological society. The phrase "eclipse of God" is Buber's alternative to the Nietzschean "death of God." Buber's notion of "eclipse" suggests that, with the passing of an age in which the light of God is blocked, there will again be the possibility of intimate contact with the absolute before whom we are placed. True, the reality of God has been undermined in the metaphysical and moral consciousness of many sophisticated people, but the vitality of the religious impulse on other levels of society cannot be denied and the presence of God may resurface in surprising forms and ways.

For Buber, the crucial error is to suppose that all encounters with God are human self-encounters. In "Religion and Modern Thinking," Buber singles out the German philosopher Martin Heidegger, the French existentialist writer Jean-Paul Sartre, and the Swiss psychoanalyst Carl Gustav Jung as refusing to accept the genuine existence of an absolute of non-human origin. For all his brilliant discussion of the nature of Being as such, Heidegger remains entrapped in a modern subjectivity that prevents confrontation with the divine. Heidegger's "cognitive clarification of the meaning of words such as God or the Holy" leads only to a "new procession of images." A divine which can be "magically" conjured up in the analysis of Being as manifested through man is, for Buber, not divine being, certainly not the eternal Thou who "disconcerts and enraptures" us and with whom we can enter into a dialogical relationship. Buber suggests Heidegger's approach allowed him to succumb to a false, demonic holiness which responsible men reject as delusion. (Buber is alluding to Heidegger's support in 1933 for Hitler as "the present and future German reality and its law.")

Heidegger, at least, held out the possibility of a new "appearance of God and the gods"; Jean-Paul Sartre concluded from the apparent "silence" of God in modern times that God does not exist or, at any rate, could not exist for modern man. For Sartre, man will regain the freedom he once ascribed to God only by recognizing himself as the being who creates his own values. Again, Buber contrasts his notion of I-Thou with Sartre's notion of the utter subjectivity of human existence. "Sartre has started from the 'silence' of God without asking himself what part our not hearing and our not having heard has played in that silence." Buber insists that one can accept a meaning and value only if they have been revealed to one, not, as Sartre avers, if one has freely chosen or invented them.

In dealing with Carl Gustav Jung, Buber concentrates on the metaphysical implications of Jung's psychology of religion. Granted, Jung had rejected the Freudian reduction of psychic processes to sex and death instincts and of religion to infantile longings. Jung's depth psychology treated religious symbolism with immense respect, and he devoted considerable attention to mysticism, mythical archetypes, and ancient views of the structure of selfhood. However, Buber faults Jung for overstepping the boundaries of psychology when he posits that religion has a living tie only to psychical events, not to a reality transcendent of the human soul. Buber insists that the soul cannot make a metaphysical assertion solely out of its own creative power, even if the "soul" we are referring to is the collective unconscious of the whole human race. Jung's notion of God as an "autonomous psychic content" is for Buber yet another instance of an inability to grasp an absolute which exists apart from man. Citing Jung's early writings, Buber suggests that his insistence on the self as a unification of opposites (feminine and masculine, light and dark, good and evil) is a modern version of ancient *gnosis*, the pagan mysticism which claimed to possess knowledge of life's greatest mysteries without acknowledging the true stance of faith toward ultimate mystery. Jung's modernized *gnosis* is, for Buber, a denial of the actual, imageless other in revelation—in effect a deification of human instincts.

Appended to the essays in *Eclipse of God* is Buber's rejoinder to Jung's reply to him. In the rejoinder, Buber offers the following description of revelation:

> [T]he human substance is melted by the spiritual fire which visits it, and there now breaks forth from it a word, a statement, which is human in its meaning and form, human conception and human speech, and yet witnesses to Him who stimulated it and to His will. We are revealed to ourselves—and cannot express it otherwise than as something revealed.

Revelation is not merely self-discovery, just as the good is not merely a human invention and God is not merely a human projection. Only by holding fast to the experienced reality of the intrapersonal other, and in no other manner, can we skirt the modern abyss of meaninglessness.

In his criticism of Nietzsche, Heidegger, Sartre, Jung, and

others, Buber stops short of offering a philosophical context for faith in God as the eternal Thou. Indeed, he denies the very possibility of treating God in objective terms (we saw that this was an important element of his critique of Hermann Cohen). His solution to the crisis of faith is simply "pointing to" the eternal Thou. Yet in "Religion and Philosophy" Buber affirms that philosophy can take us on "cogitative voyages of discovery." The I and Thou are said by Buber to subsist in Being itself—but how?

In the last analysis, *Eclipse of God* runs up against a central problem of philosophy since Kant: how to reunite subject and object, knower and known, phenomenon and noumenon. The problem hits home with especial poignancy because the objective world with which Buber is preoccupied is not physical nature but human nature. Buber singles out for rebuttal thinkers who, as he remarks, are unmoved by the dual nature of man as a being "brought forth" from below (the realms of physical and human nature) and set alongside existing beings in the world, yet a being "sent" from above (the realm of existential meeting), positioned over against absolute being before which we stand. Perhaps it was Buber's weakness that, for all his poetic eloquence, he did not engage in more rigorous analysis of the intrasubjective, di-polar nature of consciousness; one suspects that this could have been done without falling into the peril of absolutizing the autonomy of philosophy that he warned against so strongly. But likewise it was Buber's strength that he accepted the intellectual risk of faith, while rejecting ideology and orthodoxy. Holding on to God in this manner was yet another aspect of the openness and acceptance of risk he espoused.

Where does Buber fit in modern literature and religion? Is

he a poet, a philosopher, a sage? Perhaps he is best seen as a sage who is something of an Israelite prophet: in Buberian terms, Buber is a modern version of a biblical prophet whose calling it was to remind the listener repeatedly of a simple message, easily forgotten. Buber's message is that the listener must recognize himself as God addresses him, and that only then is he fully human.

Robert M. Seltzer

I

Prelude: Report on Two Talks

I SHALL tell about two talks. One apparently came to a conclusion, as only occasionally a talk can come, and yet in reality remained unconcluded; the other was apparently broken off and yet found a completion such as rarely falls to the lot of discussions.

Both times it was a dispute about God, about the concept and the name of God, but each time of a very different nature.

On three successive evenings I spoke at the adult folkschool of a German industrial city on the subject "Religion as Reality." What I meant by that was the simple thesis that "faith" is not a feeling in the soul of man but an entrance into reality, an entrance into the *whole* reality without reduction and curtailment. This thesis is simple but it contradicts the usual way of thinking. And so three evenings were necessary to make it clear, and not merely three lectures but also three discussions which followed the lectures. At these discussions I was struck by something which bothered me. A large part of the audience was evidently made up of workers but none of them spoke up. Those who spoke and raised questions, doubts, and reflections were for the most part students (for the city had a famous old university). But all kinds of other circles were also represented; the workers alone remained silent. Only at the conclusion of the third evening was this silence, which had by now become painful for me, explained. A young worker came up to me and said: "Do you know, we can't speak in there, but if you would meet with us to-morrow, we could talk together the whole time." Of course I agreed.

The next day was a Sunday. After dinner I came to the agreed place and now we talked together well into the evening. Among the workers was one, a man no longer young, whom I was drawn to look at again and again because he listened as one who really wished to hear. Real listening has become rare in our time. It is found most often among workers, who are not indeed concerned about the person speaking, as is so often the case with the *bourgeois* public, but about what he has to say. This man had a curious face. In an old Flemish altar picture representing the adoration of the shepherds one of them, who stretches out his arms toward the manger, has such a face. The man in front of me did not look as if he might have any desire to do the same; moreover, his face was not open like that in the picture. What was notable about him was that he heard and pondered, in a manner as slow as it was impressive. Finally, he opened his lips as well. "I have had the experience," he explained slowly and impressively, repeating a saying which the astronomer Laplace is supposed to have used in conversation with Napoleon, "that I do not need this hypothesis 'God' in order to be quite at home in the world." He pronounced the word "hypothesis" as if he had attended the lectures of the distinguished natural scientist who had taught in that industrial and university city and had died shortly before. Although he did not reject the designation "God" for his idea of nature, that naturalist spoke in a similar manner whether he pursued zoology or *Weltanschauung*.

The brief speech of the man struck me; I felt myself more deeply challenged than by the others. Up till then we had certainly debated very seriously, but in a somewhat relaxed way; now everything had suddenly become severe and hard. How should I reply to the man? I pondered awhile in the now severe atmosphere. It came to me that I must shatter the security of his *Weltanschauung*, through which he thought of a "world" in which one "felt at home." What sort of a world was it? What we were accustomed to call world was the "world of the senses," the world in which there exists vermilion and grass green, C major and B minor, the taste of apple and of wormwood. Was this world anything other than the meeting of our own senses with those unapproachable events about whose essential definition physics always troubles itself in vain? The red that we saw was neither there in the "things," nor here in the "soul." It at times flamed up and glowed just so long as a red-perceiving eye and a red-engendering "oscillation" found themselves over against each other. Where then was the world and its security? The unknown "objects" there, the apparently so well-known and yet not graspable "subjects" here, and the actual and still so evanescent meeting of both, the "phenomena"—was that not already three worlds which could no longer be comprehended from one alone? How could we in our thinking place together these worlds so divorced from one another? What was the being that gave this "world," which had become so questionable, its foundation?

When I was through a stern silence ruled in the now twilit room. Then the man with the shepherd's face raised his heavy lids, which had been lowered the whole time, and said slowly and impressively, "You are right."

I sat in front of him dismayed. What had I done? I had led the man to the threshold beyond which there sat enthroned the majestic image which the great physicist, the

great man of faith, Pascal, called the God of the Philosophers. Had I wished for that? Had I not rather wished to
lead him to the other, Him whom Pascal called the God of
Abraham, Isaac, and Jacob, Him to whom one can say Thou?

It grew dusk, it was late. On the next day I had to depart.
I could not remain, as I now ought to do; I could not enter
into the factory where the man worked, become his comrade,
live with him, win his trust through real life-relationship,
help him to walk with me the way of the creature who
accepts the creation. I could only return his gaze.

Some time later I was the guest of a noble old thinker. I
had once made his acquaintance at a conference where he
gave a lecture on elementary folk-schools and I gave one
on adult folk-schools. That brought us together, for we were
united by the fact that the word "folk" has to be understood
in both cases in the same all-embracing sense. At that time
I was happily surprised at how the man with the steel-grey
locks asked us at the beginning of his talk to forget all that
we believed we knew about his philosophy from his books.
In the last years, which had been war years, reality had been
brought so close to him that he saw everything with new
eyes and had to think in a new way. To be old is a glorious
thing when one has not unlearned what it means *to begin*,
this old man had even perhaps first learned it thoroughly in
old age. He was not at all young, but he was old in a young
way, knowing how to begin.

He lived in another university city situated in the west.
When the theology students of that university invited me to
speak about prophecy, I stayed with the old man. There was
a good spirit in his house, the spirit that wills to enter life
and does not prescribe to life where it shall let it in.

One morning I got up early in order to read proofs. The evening before I had received galley proof of the preface of a book of mine, and since this preface was a statement of faith, I wished to read it once again quite carefully before it was printed. Now I took it into the study below that had been offered to me in case I should need it. But here the old man already sat at his writing-desk. Directly after greeting me he asked me what I had in my hand, and when I told him, he asked whether I would not read it aloud to him. I did so gladly. He listened in a friendly manner but clearly astonished, indeed with growing amazement. When I was through, he spoke hesitatingly, then, carried away by the importance of his subject, ever more passionately. "How can you bring yourself to say 'God' time after time? How can you expect that your readers will take the word in the sense in which you wish it to be taken? What you mean by the name of God is something above all human grasp and comprehension, but in speaking about it you have lowered it to human conceptualization. What word of human speech is so misused, so defiled, so desecrated as this! All the innocent blood that has been shed for it has robbed it of its radiance. All the injustice that it has been used to cover has effaced its features. When I hear the highest called 'God,' it sometimes seems almost blasphemous."

The kindly clear eyes flamed. The voice itself flamed. Then we sat silent for awhile facing each other. The room lay in the flowing brightness of early morning. It seemed to me as if a power from the light entered into me. What I now answered, I cannot to-day reproduce but only indicate.

"Yes," I said, "it is the most heavy-laden of all human words. None has become so soiled, so mutilated. Just for this reason I may not abandon it. Generations of men have laid the

burden of their anxious lives upon this word and weighed it
to the ground; it lies in the dust and bears their whole burden.
The races of man with their religious factions have torn the
word to pieces; they have killed for it and died for it, and it
bears their finger-marks and their blood. Where might I
find a word like it to describe the highest! If I took the
purest, most sparkling concept from the inner treasure-
chamber of the philosophers, I could only capture thereby an
unbinding product of thought. I could not capture the
presence of Him whom the generations of men have honoured
and degraded with their awesome living and dying. I do
indeed mean Him whom the hell-tormented and heaven-
storming generations of men mean. Certainly, they draw
caricatures and write 'God' underneath; they murder one
another and say 'in God's name.' But when all madness and
delusion fall to dust, when they stand over against Him in the
loneliest darkness and no longer say 'He, He' but rather sigh
'Thou,' shout 'Thou,' all of them the one word, and when
they then add 'God,' is it not the real God whom they all
implore, the One Living God, the God of the children of
man? Is it not He who *hears* them? And just for this reason
is not the word 'God,' the word of appeal, the word which
has become a *name*, consecrated in all human tongues for all
times? We must esteem those who interdict it because they
rebel against the injustice and wrong which are so readily
referred to 'God' for authorization. But we may not give it
up. How understandable it is that some suggest we should
remain silent about the 'last things' for a time in order that
the misused words may be redeemed! But they are not to be
redeemed *thus*. We cannot cleanse the word 'God' and we
cannot make it whole; but, defiled and mutilated as it is, we

can raise it from the ground and set it over an hour of great care."

It had become very light in the room. It was no longer dawning, it was light. The old man stood up, came over to me, laid his hand on my shoulder and spoke: "Let us be friends." The conversation was completed. For where two or three are truly together, they are together in the name of God.

God – the word

Jews. Do not depict God
      Any name of God is a Fake God
      Suc. Relig

II

Religion and Reality

THE RELATIONSHIP between religion and reality prevailing in a given epoch is the most accurate index of its true character. In some periods, that which men "believe in" as something absolutely independent of themselves is a reality with which they are in a living relation, although they well know that they can form only a most inadequate representation of it. In other periods, on the contrary, this reality is replaced by a varying representation that men "have" and therefore can handle, or by only a residue of the representation, a concept which bears only faint traces of the original image.

Men who are still "religious" in such times usually fail to realize that the relation conceived of as religious no longer exists between them and a reality independent of them, but has existence only within the mind—a mind which at the same time contains hypostatized images, hypostatized "ideas."

Concomitantly there appears, more or less clearly, a certain type of person, who thinks that this is as it should be: in the opinion of this person, religion has never been anything but an intra-psychic process whose products are "projected" on a plane in itself fictitious but vested with reality by the soul. Cultural epochs, such men say, can be classified according to the imaginative strength of this projection; but in the end, man, having attained to clear knowledge, must recognize that every alleged colloquy with the divine was only a soliloquy, or rather a conversation between various strata of the self.

Thereupon, as a representative of this school in our time has done, it becomes necessary to proclaim that God is "dead." Actually, this proclamation means only that man has become incapable of apprehending a reality absolutely independent of himself and of having a relation with it—incapable, moreover, of imaginatively perceiving this reality and representing it in images, since it eludes direct contemplation. For the great images of God fashioned by mankind are born not of imagination but of real encounters with real divine power and glory. Man's capacity to apprehend the divine in images is lamed in the same measure as is his capacity to experience a reality absolutely independent of himself.

2

The foregoing naturally does not mean that a given concept of God, a conceptual apprehension of the divine, necessarily impairs the concrete religious relationship. Everything depends on the extent to which this concept of God can do justice to the reality which it denotes, do justice to it as a reality. The more abstract the concept, the more does it need to be balanced by the evidence of living experience, with which it is intimately bound up rather than linked in an intellectual system. The further removed a concept seems from anthropomorphism, the more it must be organically completed by an expression of that immediacy and, as it were, bodily nearness which overwhelm man in his encounters with the divine, whether they fill him with awe, transport him with rapture, or merely give him guidance. Anthropomorphism always reflects our need to preserve the concrete quality evidenced in the encounter; yet even this need is not its true root: it is in the encounter itself that we are confronted with something compellingly anthropomorphic, something demanding reciprocity, a primary Thou. This is true of those moments of our daily life in which we become aware of the reality that is absolutely independent of us, whether it be as power or as glory, no less than of the hours of great revelation of which only a halting record has been handed down to us.

We find an all-important example of the necessary supplementation of a genuine concept of God by an interpretation of what man experiences humanly, occurring just a little before the dawn of our own era, in the doctrine of Spinoza. In his theory of the divine attributes he seems to have undertaken the greatest anti-anthropomorphic effort ever essayed by the human spirit. He designates the number of the attributes of the divine substance as infinite. However, he gives names to only two of these, "extension" and "thought"—in other words, the cosmos and the spirit. Thus everything given us, both from without and within ourselves, taken together, accounts for only two of the infinite number of the attributes of God. This proposition of Spinoza's implies, among other things, a warning against identifying God with a "spiritual principle," as has been attempted particularly in our own era with ever greater insistence; for even the spirit is only one of the angelic forms, so to speak, in which God manifests Himself. However, despite the abstractness of the concept, the greatness of God is here expressed in an incomparably vivid way.

Nevertheless, this highest concept of God would have remained confined to the sphere of discursive thinking, and divorced from religious actuality, if Spinoza had not introduced into his doctrine an element which for all that it is intended to be purely "intellectual," is necessarily based on the experience that by its very nature draws man out of the domain of abstract thinking and puts him in actual relation with the real, namely, love. In this, although his exposition here is as strictly conceptual as everywhere else, Spinoza actually starts not from a concept but from a concrete fact, without which the conceptual formulation would have been impossible—and that fact is that there are men who love God (regardless of whether they are many or few, Spinoza himself obviously knew this fact from his own experience). He conceived of their love of God as God's love of Himself, actualized by His creation, and encompassing man's love of God as well as God's love of man. Thus God—the very God among the infinity of whose attributes nature and spirit are only two —loves, and since His love becomes manifest in our love of Him the divine love must be of the same essence as human love. In this way the most extreme anti-anthropomorphism evolves into a sublime anthropomorphism. Here too we end up by recognizing that we have encountered the reality of God; it is truly an encounter, for it takes place here in the realization of the identity (*unum et idem*) of His love and ours, although we, finite natural and spiritual beings, are in no wise identical with Him, who is infinite.

3

Spinoza began with propositions stating that God is, that He exists not as a spiritual principle which has no being except in the mind of him who thinks it, but as a reality, a self-subsisting reality absolutely independent of our existence; this he expresses in the concept of substance. But he concluded with propositions implying that this God stands in a living relationship to us, and we in a living relationship to him. Spinoza includes these two aspects in the one concept of God's intellectual love, and the adjective "intellectual" is to be construed in the light of the anti-anthropomorphic tendency of this philosopher, who was endeavouring to put an end to the human disposition to conceive images of God. Thus he aimed to give greater stringency to the Biblical prohibition, without, however, impairing the reality of the relation between God and man. He failed to avoid this impairment solely because he recognized only the supreme aspect of the relation, but not its core, the dialogue between God and man—the divine voice speaking in what befalls man, and man answering in what he does or forbears to do. However, Spinoza clearly stated his intention.

The thinking of our time is characterized by an essentially different aim. It seeks, on the one hand, to preserve the idea of the divine as the true concern of religion, and, on the other hand, to destroy the reality of the idea of God and thereby also the reality of our relation to Him. This is done in many ways, overtly and covertly, apodictically and hypothetically, in the language of metaphysics and of psychology.

An argument against Spinoza, which long remained unknown, and to which insufficient attention is paid even to-day, was formulated at the beginning of our era. It is a proposition found (together with several variants) in the remarkable notes set down by Kant in his old age: "God is not an external substance, but only a moral condition within us." It is true that Kant did not stop with this proposition. In the course of his restless search he propounded diametrically opposite theses in the same notes, but the reader who does not shrink from the arduous labour of reading them will nevertheless recognize that this is what Kant ultimately sought and tried to apprehend—a God who would meet the requirement of the philosopher's earlier "postulate of practical reason," a God who would overcome the contradiction between the imperative, which is unconditional, and any immanent justification, which is conditional; a God who is "the source of all moral obligation."

The fact that a God who is nothing but a condition within us cannot meet this requirement, that only an absolute can give the quality of absoluteness to an obligation, is the spur of Kant's restlessness. He had tried to avoid this fundamental difficulty in his moral philosophy by putting human society in place of the individual man, believing that the continued existence of this society depends upon the moral principle. But do we not discover, in the depth of any genuine solitude, that even beyond all social existence—nay, precisely in this realm—there is a conflict between good and evil, between fulfillment and failure to fulfil the purpose embodied in us, in this individual being? And yet I am constitutionally incapable of conceiving of myself as the ultimate source of moral approval or disapproval of myself, as surety for the absoluteness that I, to be sure, do not possess, but nevertheless imply with respect to this yes or no. The encounter with the original voice, the original source of yes or no, cannot be replaced by any self-encounter.

<h3 style="text-align:center">4</h3>

Understandably, the thinking of the era, in its effort to make God unreal, has not contented itself with reducing Him to a moral principle. The philosophers who followed Kant have tried essentially to reinstate the absolute, conceived of as existing not "within us," or at least not only within us. The traditional term "God" is to be preserved for the sake of its profound overtones, but in such a way that any connection it may have with our concrete life, as a life exposed to the manifestations of God, must become meaningless. The reality of a vision or a contact that directly determines our existence, which was a fundamental certainty to thinkers such as Plato and Plotinus, Descartes and Leibniz, is no longer found in the world of Hegel (if we disregard his youthful works, which have a completely different orientation). "The spiritual principle, that which we call God," and which "alone is real," is, by its nature, accessible only to reason, not to the whole of man as he lives his concrete life. The radical abstraction, with which philosophizing begins for Hegel, ignores the existential reality of the I and of the Thou, together with that of everything else. According to Hegel, the absolute—universal reason, the Idea, i.e., "God"—uses everything that exists and develops in nature and in history, including everything that relates to man, as an instrument of its, i.e., God's, self-realization and perfect self-awareness; but God never enters into a living, direct relation to us, nor does He vouchsafe us such a relation to Him.

At the same time, however, Hegel takes a peculiarly ambivalent attitude toward Spinoza's *amor Dei*. "The life of God and of the divine element," he says, "might be described as love in love with itself" ("*ein Spielen der Liebe mit sich selbst*"). But he adds at once, "This idea degenerates to mere edification and even insipidity if it does not include the seriousness, the pain, the patience, and the labour of the negative." For Hegel, it follows from this quite correct insight (which, it is true, does not at all apply to Spinoza's thought) that God Himself must be drawn into the dialectical process, in which negations emerge in order to be transcended. But thereby the concrete *encounter* between God and the contradiction, as it is documented with human existence, personal and historical, is relegated to the domain of fiction. The substance which, from among the infinity of its attributes, reveals to us only two, nature and spirit, and yet lets its infinite love shine in our finite love, here becomes the subject of an absolute process encompassing nature and spirit, which in this very process "achieves its truth, its consciousness of itself" in "an irresistible urge." In this process, in which the use of universal reason "mobilizes the passions for its own purposes," as Hegel puts it, "individuals are sacrificed and surrendered." The basic theme of all religions, which even so-called atheistic philosophies could only vary, the dramatic conflict between limited and unlimited being, is extinguished, because it is replaced by the exclusive rule of a universal spirit wrestling with and for itself, using everything as a means and consuming everything. Hegel, who wanted to preserve religion by renewing its form, by amending "revealed" (*offenbarte*) religion and transforming it into "manifest" (*offenbare*) religion, has denuded it of reality for the era now closing. "There is no longer anything mysterious about God," he says of this stage of development which he regards as the highest. Nothing mysterious indeed, except that what is here and now called God can no longer be for man that God which he encounters, both deeply mysterious and manifest, in his despairs and in his raptures.

5

Nietzsche's saying that God is dead, that we have slain Him, dramatically sums up the end situation of the era. But even more eloquent than this proclamation, which recapitulates a proposition of Hegel* with a change of accent and

* The connection has recently been pointed out by Heidegger. Hegel, in his essay "Faith and Knowledge," written in 1802, sought to express the essence of the feeling "on which the religion of the modern era rests" in the words, "God himself is dead." He refers in explanation to Pascal's phrase, "the lost God." But these three expressions actually mark three very different stages on one road.

meaning, are the attempts to fill the horizon that has been declared empty. I shall mention here only two of the most important of these attempts.

Bergson's point of departure is the fact of the *effort créateur que manifeste la vie*. This *effort*, he says, "is of God (*est de Dieu*), if it is not God Himself." The second part of the sentence nullifies the first. An effort, i.e., a process, or the preliminary forms of a process, cannot be named God, without making the concept of God utterly meaningless. Further, and most especially, the crucial religious experiences of man do not take place in a sphere in which creative energy operates without contradiction, but in a sphere in which evil and good, despair and hope, the power of destruction and the power of rebirth, dwell side by side. The divine force which man actually encounters in life does not hover above the demonic, but penetrates it. To confine God to a producing function is to remove Him from the world in which we live—a world filled with burning contradictions, and with yearning for salvation.

The conception represented by Heidegger is of an essentially different kind. Unlike Bergson, he does not aim at a new concept of God. He accepts Nietzsche's statement about the death of God and interprets it. This interpretation is doubtless correct to some extent. He holds the sentence "God is slain" to mean that contemporary man has shifted the concept of God from the realm of objective being to the "immanence of subjectivity." Indeed, specifically modern thought can no longer endure a God who is not confined to man's subjectivity, who is not merely a "supreme value," and, as we have seen, this thought leads us down a path which although by no means straight, is ultimately unmistakable. But then Heidegger goes on to say: "The slaying means the

elimination of the self-subsisting suprasensual world by man."
This sentence likewise, taken by itself, is correct, but it leads
to crucial problems that neither Nietzsche—if Heidegger
interprets him correctly—nor Heidegger has perceived or
acknowledged. By the "self-subsisting suprasensual world"
Heidegger means "the highest ends, the foundations and
principles of the existent, the ideals, as well as the suprasensual, God and the gods." But the living God who ap-
proaches and addresses an individual in the situations of real
life is not a component part of such a suprasensual world;
His place is no more there than it is in the sensible world, and
whenever man nonetheless has to interpret encounters with
Him as self-encounters, man's very structure is destroyed.
This is the portent of the present hour.

Heidegger rightfully looks upon this hour as an hour of
night. Thus he refers to a verse of Hölderlin, the great poet
to whose work he has devoted some of his most important
interpretative writings. Hölderlin says:

> *Aber weh! es wandelt in Nacht, es wohnt, wie im Orkus,*
> *Ohne Goettliches unser Geschlecht.*

(But alas! our generation walks in night, dwells as in Hades,
without the divine.)

It is true that Heidegger holds out the promise, even
though only as a possibility, of an intellectual transformation
from which day may dawn again, and then "the appearing of
God and the gods may begin again." But this coupling of an
absolute singular with an iridescent plural has a ring different
from that of the verses in which Hölderlin a century and a
half ago praised God and His manifestations in the active
forces of nature, i.e., the gods. To-day, when we are faced
by the question of our destiny, the question as to the essen-

tial difference between all subjectivity and that which transcends it, the juxtaposition of such a singular and such a plural seems to indicate that after the imageless era a new procession of images may begin—images of God and images of gods, images of God and gods together—without man's again experiencing and accepting his real encounters with the divine as such. But without the truth of the encounter, all images are illusion and self-deception. And who would dare, in this hour when all speech must have a deadly seriousness, to juxtapose God and the gods on the plane of the real encounter? Indeed, there was once a time when a man invoking a god in true dedication to him, really meant God Himself, the divinity of God, manifesting itself to him as a force or a form, at that moment and in that place. But this time is no longer. And even Hölderlin, when, associating singular and plural, said, *der Goetter Gott*, "the God of the gods," meaning not merely the most high of the gods, but Him whom the "gods" themselves worship as their god.

6

Eclipse of the light of heaven, eclipse of God—such indeed is the character of the historic hour through which the world is passing. But it is not a process which can be adequately accounted for by instancing the changes that have taken place in man's spirit. An eclipse of the sun is something that occurs between the sun and our eyes, not in the sun itself. Nor does philosophy consider us blind to God. Philosophy holds that we lack to-day only the spiritual orientation which can make possible a reappearance "of God and the gods," a new procession of sublime images. But when, as in this instance, something is taking place between heaven and earth, one misses everything when one insists on discovering within earthly thought the power that unveils the mystery. He who refuses to submit himself to the effective reality of the transcendence as such—our *vis-à-vis*—contributes to the human responsibility for the eclipse.

Assume that man has now fully brought about "the elimination of the self-subsisting suprasensual world," and that the principles and the ideals which have characterized man in any way, to any extent, no longer exist. His true *vis-à-vis*, which, unlike principles and ideals, cannot be described as It, but can be addressed and reached as Thou, may be eclipsed for man during the process of elimination; yet this *vis-à-vis* lives intact behind the wall of darkness. Man may even do away with the name "god," which after all implies a possessive, and which, if the possessor rejects it, i.e., if there is no longer a "God of man," has lost its *raison d'être:* yet He who is denoted by the name lives in the light of His eternity. But we, "the slayers," remain dwellers in darkness, consigned to death.

According to a Jewish legend, Adam and Eve, when they rejected God on the day of their creation and were driven out of the Garden, saw the sun set for the first time. They were terrified, for they could interpret this phenomenon only as a sign that the world was to sink back into chaos because of their guilt. Both of them wept, sitting face to face, the whole night through, and they underwent a change of heart. Then morning dawned. Adam rose, caught a unicorn, and offered it as a sacrifice in place of himself.

III

Religion and Philosophy

THE DIFFICULTY of making a radical distinction between the spheres of philosophy and religion, and, at the same time, the correct way of overcoming this difficulty, appear most clearly to us when we contrast two figures who are representative of the two spheres—Epicurus and Buddha.

Not only does Epicurus teach that there are gods, that is to say, immortal and perfect beings who live in the spaces between the worlds and yet are without power over the world or interest in it, but he also holds that one should worship these gods through pious representations of them and through the traditional rites, especially devout and fitting sacrifices. He says that he himself worships and sacrifices, but then cites the words of a character from a comedy: "I have sacrificed to gods who take no notice of me." Here is a kind of dogma and also a cultic practice, and yet clearly a philosophical rather than a religious attitude.

Buddha treats the gods of popular belief, so far as he deigns to mention them at all, with calm and considered goodwill, not unmixed with irony. These gods are, to be sure, powerful, and, unlike the gods of Epicurus, concerned with the human world. But they are bound like men by the chain of desire, heavenly figures entangled, even as men, in the "wheel of births." One may worship them, but the legends consistently picture them as paying homage to him, the Buddha, the "Awakened One," freed and freeing from the wheel of births. On the other hand, Buddha knows a genuinely divine, an "Unborn, Unoriginated, Uncreated." He knows it only in this wholly negative designation, and he refuses to make any assertions about it. Yet he stands related to it with his whole being. Here is neither proclamation nor worship of a deity, yet unmistakable religious reality.

2

Thus the personal manifestation of the divine is not decisive for the genuineness of religion. What is decisive is that I relate myself to the divine as to Being which is over against me, though *not* over against me *alone*. Complete inclusion of the divine in the sphere of the human self abolishes its divinity. It is not necessary to know something about God in order really to believe in Him: many true believers know how to talk *to* God but not *about* Him. If one dares to turn toward the unknown God, to go to meet Him, to call to Him, Reality is present. He who refuses to limit God to the transcendent has a fuller conception of Him than he who does so limit Him. But he who confines God within the immanent means something other than Him.

The radical difference between the two becomes clear when one compares religious speech in Aeschylus with that in Euripides. In *Agamemnon* the chorus says:

> Zeus, whoever he is,
> If it pleases him so to be called,
> With this name I invoke him.

How the passage, "whoever he is," is to be understood is shown by a fragment from the same poet that expresses his feelings in a paradox:

> Zeus is all and what is more than all.

Here immanence is united with transcendence. But in connection with the following passage, "If it pleases him so to be called," the scholiast rightly refers to the sentence in Plato's *Cratylus:* "We know neither the nature nor the true names of the gods." The next sentence explains that just for this reason we address them in prayer by the names they like.

In the *Trojan Women* of Euripides, on the other hand, the old queen calls upon Zeus in the following manner:

> O Foundation of the earth and above it throned,
> Whoever thou art, beyond our mind's poor grasp,
> Whether Zeus or Fate or spirit of men,
> I implore thee.

Despite the resemblance of the begining to the fragment of Aeschylus, the religious situation is abolished by the total immanence which is considered in what follows as one of the possibilities. As if one could pray to the "spirit of men"! Fragments of another tragedy of Euripides show us further what is meant. One of them says:

> We are the slaves of gods, whatever gods may be.

and another reads:

> Zeus, whoever Zeus indeed may be,—
> Only through hearsay know I aught of him.

It is a decisively significant way which leads from the "whoever he is" of Aeschylus to the seemingly similar "whoever Zeus indeed may be" of the last of the great tragedians. It is, of course, not the poet who speaks here but his characters, yet they unquestionably express the actual inner situation of his life.

It is the situation of the man who no longer experiences

the divine as standing over against him. It does not matter whether he does not dare or is unable to experience it as such. Since he has removed himself from it existentially, he no longer knows it as standing over against him. Although the chorus of Aeschylus also speaks of God in the third person, it makes a genuine invocation from human to divine being. On the other hand, in the pathos of Hecuba, despite its threefold saying of "Thou," no true Thou is in reality implied.

Protagoras once remarked that he could ascertain neither that gods exist nor that they do not, for the discovery is hindered by the mysteriousness of the subject and the brevity of human life. This famous saying translates the situation into the language of philosophical consciousness, but it is a consciousness which is strongly conditioned by the time in which Protagoras lived. For this particular consciousness, which caught up and absorbed all that was absolute in the mirror of a universal relativism, the question about the gods had become merely the question whether it was possible to ascertain their existence. To the great thinkers of the preceding age this question would have appeared meaningless. In Heraclitus' saying, "Here also are gods," the word "also" is a strong indication of the existence of immediately present divine being. And when he explains that the One which alone is wise wishes and does not wish to be called by the name of Zeus, he has given philosophical expression to an original relation between religion and philosophy as that between the meeting with the divine and its objectification in thought. The dissolution of this relation is proclaimed by the sophist, to whom the myths and cults of popular tradition are no longer witness and symbol of a transcendent presence, but rather only something in the nature of imagination or play. To the man who is no longer able to meet yet is as able as ever to think, the only possible religious question is whether man can ascertain the existence of the gods. This question, in the absence of any experience, must be answered in the negative. With the complete separation, however, of philosophy from religion, which latter is now, at most, of interest to philosophy only from the standpoint of the history of the human spirit, the possibility and the task of a radical distinction between the two spheres come into existence for the first time. This possibility and this task encompass, certainly, not only the epochs of separation but also those early periods in which each philosophy is still connected with a religion yet cogitative truth and reality of faith are already sharply distinguished. Indeed, it is just when we examine those early periods that many important distinguishing marks come most clearly to light.

trying to justify relation between rel. & phil.

3

All great religiousness shows us that reality of faith means living in relationship to Being "believed in," that is, unconditionally affirmed, absolute Being. All great philosophy, on the other hand, shows us that cogitative truth means making the absolute into an object from which all other objects must be derived. Even if the believer has in mind an unlimited and nameless absolute which cannot be conceived in a personal form, if he really thinks of it as existing Being which stands over against him, his belief has existential reality. Conversely, even if he thinks of the absolute as limited within personal form, if he reflects on it as on an object, he is philosophizing. Even when the "Unoriginated" is not addressed with voice or soul, religion is still founded on the duality of I and Thou. Even when the philosophical act culminates in a vision of unity, philosophy is founded on the

duality of subject and object. The duality of I and Thou
finds its fulfilment in the religious relationship; the duality of
subject and object sustains philosophy while it is carried on.
The first arises out of the original situation of the individual,
his living before the face of Being, turned toward him as he
is turned toward it. The second springs from the splitting
apart of this togetherness into two entirely distinct modes of
existence, one which is able to do nothing but observe and
reflect and one which is able to do nothing but be observed
and reflected upon. I and Thou exist in and by means of
lived concreteness; subject and object, products of abstraction, last only as long as that power is at work. The religious
relationship, no matter what different forms and constella-
tions it takes, is in its essence nothing other than the unfolding
of the existence that is lent to us. The philosophical attitude
is the product of a consciousness which conceives of itself
as autonomous and strives to become so. In philosophy the
spirit of man gathers itself by virtue of the spiritual work.
Indeed, one might say that here, on the peak of consummated
thought, spirituality, which has been disseminated throughout
the person, first becomes spiritual substance. But in religion,
when this is nothing other than simple existence which has
unfolded as a whole person standing over against eternal
Being, spirituality too becomes a part of personal wholeness.

Philosophy errs in thinking of religion as founded in a
noetical act, even if an inadequate one, and in therefore regarding the essence of religion as the knowledge of an object
which is indifferent to being known. As a result, philosophy
understands faith as an affirmation of truth lying somewhere
between clear knowledge and confused opinion. Religion, on
the other hand, insofar as it speaks of knowledge at all, does
not understand it as a noetic relation of a thinking subject

to a neutral object of thought, but rather as mutual contact, as the genuinely reciprocal meeting in the fullness of life between one active existence and another. Similarly, it understands faith as the entrance into this reciprocity, as binding oneself in relationship with an undemonstrable and unprovable, yet even so, in relationship, knowable Being, from whom all meaning comes.

4

Another attempt at demarcation, the mature attempt of modern philosophy, distinguishes between the intention of each. According to this conception, philosophy is directed toward the investigation of essence, religion toward inquiry about salvation. Now salvation is, to be sure, a genuine and proper religious category, but the inquiry into salvation differs from the investigation of essence only in the way in which it is considered. The principal tendency of religion is rather to show the essential unity of the two. This is illustrated by the Old Testament phrase, the "way of God," also preserved in the language of the Gospels. The "way of God" is by no means to be understood as a sum of prescriptions for human conduct, but rather primarily as the way of God in and through the world. It is the true sphere of the knowledge of God since it means God's becoming visible in His action. But it is at the same time the way of salvation of men since it is the prototype for the imitation of God. Similarly, the Chinese Tao, the "path" in which the world moves, is the cosmic primal meaning. But because man conforms this his life to it and practises "imitation of the Tao," it is at the same time the perfection of the soul.

Something further, however, is to be noted in that regard, namely, that as high as religion may place the inquiry into

salvation it does not regard it as the highest and the essential
intention. What is really intended in the search for salvation
is the attainment of a condition freed from intention, from
arbitrariness. The search for salvation is concerned with the
effect of salvation, but the "Way" itself is the unarbitrary.
Philosophy really means philosophizing; the realer religion
is, so much the more it means its own overcoming. It wills
to cease to be the special domain "Religion" and wills to
become life. It is concerned in the end not with specific
religious acts, but with redemption from all that is specific.
Historically and biographically, it strives toward the pure
Everyday. Religion is in the religious view the exile of man;
his homeland is unarbitrary life "in the face of God." It goes
against the realest will of religion to describe it in terms of
the special characteristics that it has developed rather than in
terms of its life-character. Religion must, of course, be described in such a way that its special characteristics do not
evaporate into universality but are instead seen as grounded
in the fundamental relation of religion to the whole of life.

5

When we look at the history of a historical religion, we see
the reoccurrence in different periods and phases of an inner
battle which remains essentially the same. It is the struggle
of the religious element against the non-religious elements
which invade it from all sides—metaphysics, gnosis, magic,
politics, etc. This medley seeks to take the place of the flowing life of faith which is renewed in the flux. It finds helpers
in myth and cult, both of which originally served only as
expression of the religious relationship. In order to preserve
its purity the religious element must combat the tendency
of this conglomerate to become autonomous and to make

itself independent of the religious life of the person. This battle is consummated in prophetic protest, heretical revolt, reformational retrenchment, and a new founding which arises through the desire to return to the original religious element. It is a struggle for the protection of lived concreteness as the meeting-place between the human and the divine. The actually lived concrete is the "moment" in its unforeseeableness and its irrecoverableness, in its undivertible character of happening but once, in its decisiveness, in its secret dialogue between that which happens and that which is willed, between fate and action, address and answer. This lived concreteness is threatened by the invasion of the extra-religious elements, and it is protected on all fronts by the religious in its unavoidable aloneness.

The religious essence in every religion can be found in its highest certainty. That is the certainty that the meaning of existence is open and accessible in the actual lived concrete, not above the struggle with reality but in it.

That meaning is open and accessible in the actual lived concrete does not mean it is to be won and possessed through any type of analytical or synthetic investigation or through any type of reflection upon the lived concrete. Meaning is to be experienced in living action and suffering itself, in the unreduced immediacy of the moment. Of course, he who aims at the experiencing of experience will necessarily miss the meaning, for he destroys the spontaneity of the mystery. Only he reaches the meaning who stands firm, without holding back or reservation, before the whole might of reality and answers it in a living way. He is ready to confirm with his life the meaning which he has attained.

Every religious utterance is a vain attempt to do justice to the meaning which has been attained. All religious expres-

sion is only an intimation of its attainment. The reply of the
people of Israel on Sinai, "We will do it, we will hear it,"
expresses the decisive with naïve and unsurpassable preg-
nancy. The meaning is found through the engagement of
one's own person; it only reveals itself as one takes part in its
revelation.

6

All religious reality begins with what Biblical religion calls
the "fear of God." It comes when our existence between
birth and death becomes incomprehensible and uncanny,
when all security is shattered through the mystery. This is
not the relative mystery of that which is inaccessible only
to the present state of human knowledge and is hence in
principle discoverable. It is the essential mystery, the inscrut-
ableness of which belongs to its very nature; it is the unknowable. Through this dark gate (which is only a gate and
not, as some theologians believe, a dwelling) the believing
man steps forth into the everyday which is henceforth
hallowed as the place in which he has to live with the
mystery. He steps forth directed and assigned to the concrete, contextual situations of his existence. That he henceforth accepts the situation as given him by the Giver is what
Biblical religion calls the "fear of God."

An important philosopher of our day, Whitehead, asks how
the Old Testament saying that the fear of God is the beginning of wisdom is to be reconciled with the New Testament
saying that God is love. Whitehead has not fully grasped the
meaning of the word "beginning." He who begins with the
love of God without having previously experienced the fear
of God, loves an idol which he himself has made, a god whom
it is easy enough to love. He does not love the real God who

Must have fear of God before
you can love God,
Religion and Philosophy 37

is, to begin with, dreadful and incomprehensible. Consequently, if he then perceives, as Job and Ivan Karamazov
perceive, that God is dreadful and incomprehensible, he is
terrified. He despairs of God and the world if God does not
take pity on him, as He did on Job, and bring him to love
Him Himself. This is presumably what Whitehead meant
when he said that religion is the passage from God the void
to God the enemy and from Him to God the companion.
That the believing man who goes through the gate of dread
is directed to the concrete contextual situations of his existence means just this: that he endures in the face of God the
reality of lived life, dreadful and incomprehensible though it
be. He loves it in the love of God, whom he has learned to
love.

For this reason, every genuine religious expression has an
open or a hidden personal character, for it is spoken out of a
concrete situation in which the person takes part as a person.
This is true also in those instances where, out of a noble
modesty, the word "I" is in principle avoided. Confucius,
who spoke of himself almost as unwillingly as of God, once
said: "I do not murmur against God, and I bear no ill will
toward men. I search here below, but I penetrate above. He
who knows me is God." Religious expression is bound to the
concrete situation.

That one accepts the concrete situation as given to him does
not, in any way, mean that he must be ready to accept that
which meets him as "God-given" in its pure factuality. He
may, rather, declare the extremest enmity toward this happening and treat its "givenness" as only intended to draw
forth his own opposing force. But he will not remove himself from the concrete situation as it actually is; he will,
instead, enter into it, even if in the form of fighting against

Religion is something concrete

it. Whether field of work or field of battle, he accepts the place in which he is placed. He knows no floating of the spirit above concrete reality; to him even the sublimest spirituality is an illusion if it is not bound to the situation. Only the spirit which is bound to the situation is prized by him as bound to the *Pneuma*, the spirit of God.

As an objection to the definition of religion which I have suggested, one might adduce the ascetic tendencies of some religions. Insofar, however, as they do not weaken the religious itself, these tendencies do not mean any turning away from the lived concrete. The disposition of life and the choice of life-elements to be affirmed has changed here. But this change is not in the direction of slackening the relation to the moment, which one is rather seeking to intensify. One desires to rescue the relation to the moment by means of asceticism because one despairs of being able to subjugate the non-ascetic elements, and hence the fullness of life, to the religious. The meaning no longer appears to him as open and attainable in the fullness of life.

The ascetic "elevation" is something entirely different from the philosophical. It is also a form of concretion, though one which is attained through reduction.

7

Philosophizing and philosophy, in contrast, begin ever anew with one's definitely looking away from his concrete situation, hence with the primary act of abstraction.

What is meant here by abstraction is simple, anthropological matter of fact and not the "radical abstraction" with which Hegel demands that the philosopher begin. Hegel can call the creation of the world an abstraction from nothing, while for us it involves precisely the establishment of that concrete reality from which the philosophizing man does and must look away. Hegel can describe "the highest being" as "pure abstraction" while the religious man, on the contrary, is certain that in the course of this his mortality he can meet God in God's very giving and in his, man's, receiving of the concrete situation. By primary abstraction we mean the inner action in which man lifts himself above the concrete situation into the sphere of precise conceptualization. In this sphere the concepts no longer serve as a means of apprehending reality, but instead represent as the object of thought being freed from the limitations of the actual.

The decisiveness of this abstraction, of this turning away, is sometimes hidden from sight when a philosopher acts as if he would and could philosophize within his concrete situation. Descartes offers us the clearest example. When we hear him talk in the first person, we feel as if we were hearing the voice of direct personal experience. But it is not so. The I in the Cartesian *ego cogito* is not the living, body-soul person whose corporality had just been disregarded by Descartes as being a matter of doubt. It is the subject of consciousness, supposedly the only function which belongs entirely to our nature. In lived concreteness, in which consciousness is the first violin but not the conductor, *this* ego is not present at all. *Ego cogito* means to Descartes, indeed, not simply "I have consciousness," but "It is I who have consciousness." *Ego cogito* is, therefore, the product of a triply abstracting reflection. Reflection, the "bending back" of a person on himself, begins by extracting from what is experienced in the concrete situation "consciousness" (*cogitatio*), which is not as such experienced there at all. It then ascertains that a subject must belong to a consciousness and calls this subject "I." In the end, it identifies the person, this living body-soul person, with that "I," that is, with the abstract and abstractly-produced subject of consciousness. Out of the "That" of the concrete situation, which embraces perceiving and that which is perceived, conceiving and that which is conceived, thinking and that which is thought, arises, to begin with, an "I think that." A subject thinks this object. Then the really indispensable "That" (or Something or It) is omitted. Now we reach the statement of the person about himself: therefore I (no longer the subject, but the living person who speaks to us) have real existence; for this existence is involved in that *ego*.

In this way Descartes sought through the method of abstraction to capture the concrete starting-point as knowledge, but in vain. Not through such a deduction but only through genuine intercourse with a Thou can the I of the living person be experienced as existing. The concrete, from which all philosophizing starts, cannot again be reached by way of philosophical abstraction; it is irrecoverable.

Philosophy is entitled, however, to proclaim and to promise as the highest reward of this necessary abstraction a looking upward—no longer a looking here—at the objects of true vision, the "ideas." This conception, prepared for by the Indian teaching of the freeing of the knower from the world of experience, is first fully developed by the Greeks. The Greeks established the hegemony of the sense of sight over the other senses, thus making the optical world into *the* world, into which the data of the other senses are now to be entered. Correspondingly, they also gave to philosophizing, which for the Indian was still only a bold attempt to catch hold of one's own self, an optical character, that is, the character of the contemplation of particular objects. The history of Greek philosophy is that of an opticizing of thought, fully clarified in Plato and perfected in Plotinus. The object of this visual thought is the universal existence or as a reality higher than existence. Philosophy is grounded on the presupposition that one sees the absolute in universals.

In opposition to this, religion, when it has to define itself philosophically, says that it means the covenant of the absolute with the particular, with the concrete. For this reason, the central event of Christian philosophy, the scholastic dispute over the reality or unreality of universals, was in essence a philosophical struggle between religion and philosophy and that is its lasting significance. In religious-sounding formulas such as Malebranche's "we see things in God" it is also philosophical abstraction that speaks; for these "things" are not those of the concrete situation but are as general as Platonic ideas ("*les idées intelligibles*"). When, on the contrary, the religious man (or Malebranche no longer as philosophical systematizer but as the religious man that he was) speaks the same sentence, he transforms it. "Things" mean now to him not archetypes or "perfect essences," but the actual exemplars, the beings and objects with which he, this bodily person, spends his life. When he ventures to say that he sees them in God, he does not speak of looking upward but of looking here. He acknowledges that meaning is open and attainable in the lived concreteness of every moment.

Plato gives us a glorious human and poetic account of the mysterious fullness of the concrete situation. He also knows gloriously how to remain silent. When, however, he explains and answers for his silence in that unforgettable passage of the seventh epistle, he starts, to be sure, from the concreteness of "life together," where "in an instant a light is kindled as from springing fire." But in order to explain he turns immediately to an exposition of the knowing of the known, meaning the universal. Standing in the concrete situation and

Religious man sees it differently "object"

even witnessing to it, man is overspanned by the rainbow of the covenant between the absolute and the concrete. If he wishes in philosophizing to fix his glance upon the white light of the absolute as the object of his knowledge, only archetypes or ideas, the transfigurations of the universal, present themselves to him. The color-free, beyond-color bridge fails to appear. Here also, in my opinion, is to be found the reason why Plato changed from the identification of the idea of the good with God, as presented in his *Republic*, to the conception appearing in the *Timaeus* of the demiurge who contemplates the Ideas.

8

Religion, however, is not allowed, even in the face of the most self-confident pride of philosophy, to remain blind to philosophy's great engagement. To this engagement necessarily belongs the actual, ever-recurring renunciation of the original relational bond, of the reality which takes place between I and Thou, of the spontaneity of the moment. Religion must know knowledge not only as a need but also as a duty of man. It must know that history moves along the way of this need and duty, that, Biblically speaking, the eating of the tree of knowledge leads out of Paradise but into the world.

The world, the world as objective and self-contained connection of all being, natural and spiritual, would not exist for us if our thinking, which develops in philosophizing, did not melt together the world-concreta which are presented to us. It would not exist if our thinking did not merge these world-concreta with one another and with all that man has ever experienced and has ever comprehended as experienceable. And spirit all the more would not genuinely exist for us as objective connection if thought did not objectify it, if spirit itself as philosophy did not objectify and unite itself. Only through the fact that philosophy radically abandoned the relation with the concrete did that amazing construction of an objective thought-continuum become possible, with a static system of concepts and a dynamic one of problems. Every man who can "think" may enter this continuum through the simple use of this ability, through a thinking comprehension of thought. Only through this is there an "objective" mutual understanding, that is, one which does not, like the religious, entail two men's each recognizing the other by the personal involvement in life which he has achieved. Instead, both fulfil a function of thought which demands no involvement in life and bear in fruitful dialectic the tension between the reciprocal ideas and problems.

The religious communication of a content of being takes place in paradox. It is not a demonstrable assertion (theology which pretends to be this is rather a questionable type of philosophy), but a pointing toward the hidden realm of existence of the hearing man himself and that which is to be experienced there and there alone. Artistic communication, which ought not remain unmentioned here, takes place in the *Gestalt*, from which a communicated content cannot be detached and given independent existence. A content of being is objectively communicable and translatable only in and through philosophy, consequently only through the objectifying elaboration of the situation.

A sceptical verdict about the ability of philosophy to lead to and contain truth is in no way here implied. The possibility of cogitative truth does not, indeed, mean a cogitative possession of being, but a cogitative real relation to being. Systems of thought are manifestations of genuine thought-relations to being made possible through abstraction. They are not mere "aspects," but rather valid documents of these cogitative voyages of discovery.

A similarity and a difference between the ways in which religion and philosophy affect the person remain to be mentioned.

In religious reality the person has concentrated himself into a whole, for it is only as a unified being that he is able to live religiously. In this wholeness thought is naturally also included as an autonomous province but one which no longer strives to absolutize its autonomy. A totalization also takes place in genuine philosophers but no unification. Instead, thinking overruns and overwhelms all the faculties and provinces of the person. In a great act of philosophizing even the finger-tips think—but they no longer feel.

9

For man the existent is either face-to-face being or passive object. The essence of man arises from this twofold relation to the existent. These are not two external phenomena but the two basic modes of existing with being. The child that calls to his mother and the child that watches his mother—or to give a more exact example, the child that silently speaks to his mother through nothing other than looking into her eyes and the same child that looks at something on the mother as at any other object—show the twofoldness in which man stands and remains standing. Something of the sort is sometimes even to be noticed in those near death. What is here apparent is the double structure of human existence itself. Because these are the two basic modes of our existence with being, they are the two basic modes of our existence in general—I-Thou and I-It. I-Thou finds its highest intensity and transfiguration in religious reality, in which unlimited Being becomes, as absolute person, my partner. I-It finds its highest concentration and illumination in philosophical knowledge. In this knowledge the extraction of the subject from the I of the immediate lived togetherness of I and It and the transformation of the It into the object detached in its essence produces the exact thinking of contemplated existing beings, yes, of contemplated Being itself.

Divine truth, according to a saying of Franz Rosenzweig, wishes to be implored "with both hands," that of philosophy and that of theology. "He who prays with the double prayer of the believer and the unbeliever," he continues, "to him it will not deny itself." But what is the prayer of the unbeliever? Rosenzweig means by this Goethe's prayer to his own destiny, a prayer which, no matter how genuine, brings to mind that of the Euripidean queen to fate or the human spirit, a prayer whose Thou is no Thou. But there is another prayer of the philosophers still farther from the Thou, and yet, it seems to me, more important.

The religious reality of the meeting with the Meeter, who shines through all forms and is Himself formless, knows no image of Him, nothing comprehensible as object. It knows only the presence of the Present One. Symbols of Him, whether images or ideas, always exist first when and insofar as Thou becomes He, and that means It. But the ground of human existence in which it gathers and becomes whole is also the deep abyss out of which images arise. Symbols of God come into being, some which allow themselves to be fixed in lasting visibility even in earthly material and some which tolerate no other sanctuary than that of the soul. Symbols supplement one another, they merge, they are set before the community of believers in plastic or theological forms. And God, so we may surmise, does not despise all these similarly and necessarily untrue images, but rather suffers that one look at Him through them. Yet they always quickly desire to be more than they are, more than signs and pointers toward Him. It finally happens ever again that they swell themselves up and obstruct the way to Him, and He removes Himself from them. Then comes round the hour of the philosopher, who rejects both the image and the God which it symbolizes and opposes to it the pure idea, which he even at times understands as the negation of all metaphysical ideas. This critical "atheism" (*Atheoi* is the name which the Greeks gave to those who denied the traditional gods) is the prayer which is spoken in the third person in the form of speech about an idea. It is the prayer of the philosopher to the again unknown God. It is well suited to arouse religious men and to impel them to set forth right across the God-deprived reality to a new meeting. On their way they destroy the images which manifestly no longer do justice to God. The spirit moves them which moved the philosopher.

IV

*The Love of God and the
Idea of Deity*

IN THOSE scribbled lines affecting us as cries of the very soul, which Pascal wrote after two ecstatic hours, and which he carried about with him until his death, sewn into the lining of his doublet, we find under the heading *Fire* the note: "God of Abraham, God of Isaac, God of Jacob—not of the philosophers and scholars."

These words represent Pascal's change of heart. He turned, not from a state of being where there is no God to one where there is a God, but from the God of the philosophers to the God of Abraham. Overwhelmed by faith, he no longer knew what to do with the God of the philosophers; that is, with the God who occupies a definite position in a definite system of thought. The God of Abraham, the God in whom Abraham had believed and whom Abraham had loved ("The entire religion of the Jews," remarks Pascal, "consisted only of the love of God"), is not susceptible of introduction into a system of thought precisely because He is God. He is beyond each and every one of those systems, absolutely and by virtue of His nature. What the philosophers describe by the name of God cannot be more than an idea. But God, "the God of Abraham," is not an idea; all ideas are absorbed in Him. Nor is that all. If I think even of a state of being in which all ideas are absorbed, and think some philosophic thought about it as an idea—then I am no longer referring to the God of Abraham. The "passion" peculiar to philosophers is, according to a hint dropped by Pascal, pride. They offer humanity their own system in place of God.

"What!" cries Pascal, "the philosophers recognized God and desired not merely that men should love him, but that they should reach their level and then stop!" It is precisely because the philosophers replace him by the image of images, the idea, that they remove themselves and remove the rest of us furthest from him. There is no alternative. One must choose. Pascal chose, during one of those all-overthrowing moments, when he felt his sick-bed prayer was answered: "To be apart from the world, divested of all things, lonely in your Presence, in order to respond to your justice with all the motions of my heart."

Pascal himself, to be sure, was not a philosopher but a mathematician, and it is easier for a mathematician to turn his back on the God of the philosophers than for a philosopher. For the philosopher, if he were really to wish to turn his back on that God, would be compelled to renounce the attempt to include God in his system in any conceptual form. Instead of including God as one theme among others, that is, as the highest theme of all, his philosophy both wholly and in part would be compelled to point toward God, without actually dealing with him. This means that the philosopher would be compelled to recognize and admit the fact that his idea of the Absolute was dissolving at the point where the Absolute *lives*; that it was dissolving at the point where the Absolute is loved; because at that point the Absolute is no longer the "Absolute" about which one may philosophize, but God.

2

Those who wish clearly to grasp the nature of the endless and hopeless struggle which lay in wait for the philosopher of the critical period should read the very long notes in Kant's unfinished posthumous work, written over a period of seven years during his old age. They reveal a scene of incomparable existential tragedy. Kant calls the principle constituting the transition to the completion of the transcendental philosophy by the name of the "Principle of Transcendental Theology"; here his concern is with the questions, "What is God?" and "Is there a God?"

Kant explains: "The function of transcendental philosophy is still unresolved: Is there a God?" As long as there was no reply to that question, the task of his philosophy was still unfulfilled; at the end of his days, when his spiritual powers were waning, it was "still unresolved." He toiled on at this problem, constantly increasing his efforts, from time to time weaving the answer, yet time and again unraveling the woof. He reached an extreme formulation: "To think Him and to believe in Him is an identical act." Furthermore, "the thought of Him is at one and the same time the belief in Him and his personality." But this faith does not result in God's becoming existent for the philosophy of the philosopher. "God is not an entity outside of me, but merely a thought within me." Or, as Kant says on another occasion, "merely a moral relation within me."

Nevertheless, He possesses a certain kind of "reality." "God is only an idea of reason, but one possessing the greatest practical internal and external reality." Yet it is obvious that this kind of reality is not adequate to make the thought about God identical with the "belief in Him and His personality." Transcendental philosophy, whose task was to ascertain whether there is a God, finally found itself compelled to state: "It is preposterous to ask whether there is a God."

The contradiction goes even deeper when Kant treats

belief from this point of view. He incidentally outlines a fundamental distinction between "to believe God" and "to believe in God." "To believe God" obviously means God's being the ideational content of one's faith. This is a deduction from the fact that "to believe in God" means in the terminology of Kant, as he himself expressly states, to believe in a living God. To believe in God means, therefore, to stand in a personal relationship to that God; a relationship in which it is possible to stand only toward a living entity.

This distinction becomes still clearer through Kant's addendum: to believe "not in an entity which is only an idol and is not a personality." It follows that a God who is not a living personality is an idol. Kant comes that close at this point to the *reality* of faith. But he does not permit its validity to stand. His system compels him decisively to restrict what he has said. The same page of manuscript contains the following passage: "The idea of God as a living God is nothing but the inescapable fate of man." But if the idea of God is only that, then it is totally impossible to "believe in God" legitimately; that is, it is impossible to stand in a personal relationship with him. Man, declares the philosopher, is compelled to believe in him the moment he thinks God. But the philosopher is compelled to withdraw the character of truth from this faith, and together with it the character of reality (any reality, that is, which is more than merely psychological). Here, apparently of necessity, that which was decisive for Pascal, as it was for Abraham, is missing; namely, the love of God.

3

But a philosopher who has been overwhelmed by faith *must* speak of love.

Hermann Cohen, the last in the series of great disciples of Kant, is a shining example of a philosopher who has been overwhelmed by faith.

Belief in God was an important point in Cohen's system of thought as early as in his youth, when it interested him as a psychological phenomenon. His explanations of "the origin of the mythology of gods" and of the "poetic act" involved in "god-creating fantasy," contained in his study on "Mythological Conceptions concerning God and Soul" which appeared in 1868 in Steinthal's periodical, *Zeitschrift fuer Voelkerpsychologie*, was an expression of this interest. Faith was there treated as relative to psychological distinction; but in the course of the development of Cohen's philosophical system faith's status as an independent concept, distinct from knowledge, was to become questionable.

In his "Ethics of Pure Will" (1904), Cohen writes: "God must not become the content of belief, if that belief is to mean something distinct from knowledge." Of the two kinds of belief which Kant distinguishes in his posthumous work, namely, "to believe God" (that is, to introduce the idea of God into a system of knowledge), and "to believe in a living God" (that is, to have a vital relationship to him as a living entity), Cohen rejects the second even more strongly than Kant. In this way he means to overcome the "great equivocality" of the word "belief." Whereas Kant saw in the idea of God only the "fate" of the human species, Cohen wishes to "separate the concept of life from the concept of God." He finds support for his argument in Maimonides (though he limited the extent of that support three years later, saying that Maimonides had been careful to distinguish between the concept of life when applied to God and the same concept when applied to man; a distinction on the part of Maimonides which entirely differs from Cohen's distinction).

God is an idea for Cohen, as he was for Kant. "We call God an idea," says Cohen, "meaning the center of all ideas, the idea of truth." God is not a personality; as such He only appears "within the confines of myth." And He is no existence at all, neither a natural existence nor a spiritual, "just as in general the idea cannot be linked with the concept of existence." The concept of God is introduced into the structure of ethical thought, because, as the idea of truth, it is instrumental in establishing the unity of nature and morality. This view of God as an idea Cohen regards as "the true religiosity," which can evolve only when every relation involving belief in a living God is shown to be problematical, and nullified. God's only place is within a system of thought. The system defends itself with stupendous vigour against the living God who is bound to make questionable its perfection, and even its absolute authority. Cohen, the thinker, defends himself against the belief which, rising out of an ancient heritage, threatens to overwhelm him. He defends himself with success; the success of the system-creator. Cohen has constructed the last home for the God of the philosophers.

And yet Cohen has been overwhelmed by faith in more exemplary fashion than any other of the contemporary philosophers, although his labours to incorporate God into a system were in no way hindered. On the contrary: from that moment his labours turned into an admirable wrestle with his own experience.

Cohen objectified the results of his succumbing to faith by merging it in his system of concepts. Nowhere in his writings does he directly state it; but the evidence is striking. When was it that the decisive change occurred?

4

The answer lies in the change that crept into Cohen's way of thinking about the love of God. It was only at a late period that Cohen, who concurrently with the development of his system was dealing in a series of essays with the heritage of the Jewish faith, gave an adequate place to the cornerstone of that faith, the love of God, the essential means by which the Jewish faith realized its full and unique value. Only three years after the "Ethics," in his important research into "Religion and Morality," whose formulations, even keener than those of the "Ethics," interdict "interest in the so-called person of God and the so-called living God," declaring that the prophets of Israel "combatted" the direct relation between man and God, do we find a new note about the love of God. "The more that the knowledge of God is simultaneously felt to be love of God, the more passionate becomes the battle for faith, the struggle for the knowledge of God and for the love of God." It is evident that at this point Cohen is beginning to approach the *vital* character of faith. Yet the love of God still remains something abstract and not given to investigation.

Once again, three years later, Cohen's short essay on "The Love of Religion" begins with the curious sentence, "The love of God is the love of religion," and its first section ends with the no less curious sentence, "The love of God is therefore the knowledge of morality." If we carefully consider the two uses of the word "is," we are able to distinguish a purpose: which is to classify something as yet unclassified but nevertheless obtruding as central; to classify it by a process of identification with something else already comprehended, and thus put it in its place; but that identification does not prove successful. All that is necessary to see this clearly is to compare the above-cited sentences with any one of the Biblical verses which enjoin or praise the love of God, which are the origin of that concept. What Cohen is enjoining and praising at this point is something essentially and qualitatively different from the love of religion and the knowledge of morality, although it includes both. Yet in Cohen's revision of his Berlin lectures of 1913-14, published in 1915 under the title, "The Concept of Religion in the System of Philosophy," he gives expression to a love which does away once and for all with that curious "is."

"If I love God," says Cohen (and this use of his of "I" touches the heart of the reader, like every genuine "I" in the work of every genuine philosopher), "then I no longer think Him . . ." (and that "no longer" is almost direct testimony) ". . . only the sponsor of earthly morals. . . ." But what? But the avenger of the poor in world history. "It is that avenger of the poor whom I love." And later, to the same effect: "I love in God the father of man." At this point "father" means the "shield and aid of the poor," for, "Man is revealed to me in the poor man."

How long a way have we come from the "love of religion"! Yet the new element in Cohen is expressed with even greater clarity and energy: "Therefore shall the love of God exceed all knowledge. . . . A man's consciousness is completely filled when he loves God. Therefore, this knowledge, which absorbs all others, is no longer merely knowledge, but love." And it is extremely logical that the Biblical commandment to love God is cited and interpreted at this point in the same connection: "I cannot love God without devoting my whole heart as living for the sake of my fellow-men, without devoting my entire soul as responsive to all the spiritual trends in the world around me, without devoting all my force to this God in His correlation with man."

At this point I wish to introduce an objection related, admittedly, not to these sentences of Cohen's, but to another that has a connection with them. Cohen speaks of the paradox "that I have to love man." "Worm that I am," he continues, "consumed by passions, cast as bait for egoism, I must nevertheless love man. If I am able to do so, and so far as I am able to do so, I shall be able to love God." Strong words these, yet the lives of many important persons controvert the last sentence. The teaching of the Bible overcomes the paradox in a precisely contrary fashion. The Bible knows that it is impossible to command the love of man. I am incapable of feeling love toward every man, though God himself command me. The Bible does not directly enjoin the love of man, but by using the dative puts it rather in the form of an *act* of love (Lev. 19:18, 34). I must act lovingly toward my *rea*, my "companion" (usually translated "my neighbour"), that is toward every man with whom I deal in the course of my life, including the *ger*, the "stranger" or "sojourner"; I must bestow the favours of love on him, I must treat him with love as one who is "like unto me." (I must love "to him"; a construction only found in these two verses in the Bible.) Of course I must love him not merely with superficial gestures but with an essential relationship. It lies within my power to will it, and so I can accept the commandment. It is not my will which gives me the emotion of love toward my "neighbour" aroused within me by my behaviour.

On the other hand, the Torah commands one to love God (Deut. 6:5; 10:12; 11:1); only in that connection does it enjoin heartfelt love of the sojourner who is one's "neighbour" (Deut. 10:19)—because God loves the sojourner. **If**

I love God, in the course of loving Him I come to love the one whom God loves, too. I can love God as God from the moment I know Him; and Israel, to whom the commandment is addressed, does know Him. Thus I can accept the injunction to love my fellow-man.

Cohen is, to be sure, actually referring to something else. For now he raises the question whether he should take offense at God's being "only an idea." "Why should I not be able," he replies, "to love ideas? What is man after all but a social idea, and yet I can love him as an individual only through and by virtue of that fact. Therefore, strictly considered, I can only love the social idea of man."

To me, it seems otherwise. Only if and because I love this or that specific man can I elevate my relation to the social idea of man into that emotional relationship involving my whole being which I am entitled to call by the name of love. And what of God? Franz Rosenzweig warned us that Cohen's idea of God should not be taken to mean that God is "only an idea" in Cohen's eyes. The warning is pertinent: Rosenzweig is right to emphasize that an idea for Cohen is not "only an idea." Yet, at the same time, we must not ignore that other "only," whose meaning is quite different indeed in Cohen's phrase, "a God who is only an idea." Let us, if we will, describe our relation to the idea of the beautiful and the idea of the good by the name of love—though in my opinion all this has content and value for the soul only in being rendered concrete and made real. But to love God differs from that relationship in essential quality. He who loves God loves Him precisely insofar as He is not "only an idea," and can love Him *because* He is not "only an idea." And I permit myself to say that though Cohen indeed thought of God as an idea, Cohen too loved Him as—God.

5

In the great work prepared after "The Concept of Religion" and posthumously published under the title of "Religion of Reason, from the Sources of Judaism," Cohen returns to this problem with even greater prominence: "How can one love an idea?"—and replies, "How can one love anything save an idea?" He substantiates his reply by saying, "For even in the love of the senses one loves only the idealized person, only the idea of the person." Yet even if it were correct that in the love of "the senses" (or more correctly, in the love which comprehends sensuality) one loves only the idealized person, that does not at all mean that nothing more than the idea of the person is loved; even the idealized person remains a person, and has not been transformed into an idea. It is only because the person whom I idealize actually exists that I can love the idealized one. Even though for Dante it was *la gloriosa donna della mia mente*, yet the decisive fact is that first he saw the real Beatrice, who set the "spirit of life" trembling in him. But does not the motive force which enables and empowers us to idealize a beloved person arise from the deepest substance of that beloved person? Is not the true idealization in the deepest sense a *discovery* of the essential self meant by God in creating the person whom I love?

"The love of men for God," says Cohen, "is the love of the moral ideal. I can love only the ideal, and I can comprehend the ideal in no other way save by loving it." Even on this level, the very highest for the philosopher who is overwhelmed by faith, he declares what the love of God is, and not what it includes. But man's love for God *is not* love of the moral ideal; it only includes that love. He who loves God only as the moral ideal is bound soon to reach the point of despair at the conduct of the world where, hour after hour, all the principles of his moral idealism are apparently contradicted. Job despairs because God and the moral ideal seem diverse to him. But He who answered Job out of the tempest is more exalted even than the ideal sphere. He is not the archetype of the ideal, but he contains the archetype. He issues forth the ideal, but does not exhaust himself in the issuing. The unity of God is not the Good; it is the Supergood. God desires that men should follow His revelation, yet at the same time He wishes to be accepted and loved in His deepest concealment. He who loves God loves the ideal and loves God more than the ideal. He knows himself to be loved by God, not by the ideal, not by an idea, but even by Him whom ideality cannot grasp, namely, by that *absolute personality* we call God. Can this be taken to mean that God "is" a personality? The absolute character of His personality, that paradox of paradoxes, prohibits any such statement. It only means that God loves as a personality and that He wishes to be loved like a personality. And if He was not a person in Himself, He, so to speak, became one in creating Man, in order to love man and be loved by him—in order to love me and be loved by me. For, even supposing that ideas can also be loved, the fact remains that persons are the only ones who love. Even the philosopher who has been overwhelmed by faith, though he afterward continue to hug his system even more closely than before, and to interpret the love between God and man as the love between an idea and a person—even he, nevertheless, testifies to the existence of a love between God and man that is basically reciprocal. That philosophy too, which, in order to preserve the Being (*esse; Sein*) of God, deprives Him of existence (*existentia; Dasein*), indicates however unintentionally the bridge standing indestructibly on the two pillars, one imperishable and the other ever crumbling, God and man.

6

Cohen once said of Kant, "What is characteristic of his theology is the non-personal *in the usual sense*, the truly spiritual principle: the sublimation of God into an idea." And he adds, "And nothing less than this is the deepest basis of the Jewish idea of God." As far as Kant is concerned, Cohen was correct in this judgment. But throughout Kant's posthumous work we can see emerging every now and then resistance to this sublimation of God into an idea; a sublimation which later even more prominently prevents in Cohen the linking of the idea with the concept of existence.

"Under the concept of God," writes Kant, "Transcendental Philosophy refers to a substance possessing the greatest existence," but he also qualifies God as "the ideal of a substance which we create ourselves." What we have in these notes, which sometimes appear chaotic, are the records of a suit at law, the last phase which the thought of the idea of God assumes for its thinker, of a suit between the two elements, "idea" and "God," which are contained in the idea of God; a suit which time and again reverts to the same point, until death cuts it short. Cohen set out to put the idea into a sequence so logical as to make it impossible for any impulse to opposition to develop. Even when overwhelmed by faith, Cohen continued the struggle to preserve this sequence. In so doing, he was of the opinion that "the deepest basis of the Jewish idea of God" was on his side. But even the deepest basis of the Jewish idea of God can be achieved only by plunging into that word by which God revealed Himself to Moses, "I shall be there." * It gives exact expression to the personal "existence" of God (not to His abstract "being"), and expression even to His living presence, which most directly of all His attributes touches the man to whom He manifests Himself. The speaker's self-designation as the God of Abraham, God of Isaac, and God of Jacob (Exod. 3:15) is indissolubly united with that manifestation of "I shall be there," and He cannot be reduced to a God of the philosophers.

But the man who says, "I love in God the father of man" has essentially already renounced the God of the philosophers in his innermost heart, even though he may not confess it to himself. Cohen did not consciously choose between the God of the philosophers and the God of Abraham, rather believing to the last that he could succeed in identifying the two. Yet his inmost heart, that force from which thought too derives its vitality, had chosen and decided for him. The identification had failed, and of necessity had to fail. For the idea of God, that masterpiece of man's construction, is only the image of images, the most lofty of all the images by which man imagines the imageless God. It is essentially repugnant to man to recognize this fact, and remain satisfied. For when man learns to love God, he senses an actuality which rises above the idea. Even if he makes the philosopher's great effort to sustain the object of his love as an object of his philosophic thought, the love itself bears witness to the existence of the Beloved.

* Exod. 3:14, part of the phrase commonly translated: "I am that I am."

V

Religion and Modern Thinking

ontology = Systematic study of being

I SHALL speak of the relation of modern thought to religion. By this I do not mean the attempts to think from the standpoint of religious reality, or to create an understanding between it and philosophy based on mutual tolerance. My subject shall rather be modern thought only insofar as it undertakes to give a verdict as to whether or under what conditions or within what limits the character of a living human reality can be ascribed to religion. We find a judgment of this sort in the ontological sense, on the one hand, in the socalled existentialism of Sartre and Heidegger, and in the psychological sense, on the other, in Jung's theory of the collective unconscious. Basic to both positions is the assumption that the outcome of the crisis in which religion has entered depends essentially upon the judgments which are made by modern ontological or psychological thought. It is this assumption that we must examine.

In naming Heidegger and Sartre together, I by no means imply that they have the same attitude toward religion. On the contrary, in this respect as in so many others they are without doubt radically dissimilar, and accordingly the reply to the one must be entirely different from the reply to the other.

Sartre proclaims his atheism; he says,[1] "The atheistic existentialism, which I represent. . . ." Among the representatives of this position he has, to be sure, included Heidegger; but Heidegger has refused to allow himself to be thus classified.

We must therefore deal with Sartre by himself. He clearly wishes his atheism to be understood as a logical consequence of his existential philosophy. We undoubtedly have here before us an atheism which is basically different from any materialistic one. That it follows, however, from an existential conception of the world, that is, from one which proceeds from the reality of human existence, cannot be substantiated.

Sartre accepts Nietzsche's cry, or better shout, "God is dead!" as a valid statement of fact. Our generation appears to him as specifically the one which has outlived God. He says once[2]—although elsewhere[3] he most emphatically asserts, as one who knows, *"Dieu n'existe pas"*—that the fact that God is dead does not mean that he does not exist nor even that he no longer exists. In place of these interpretations he presents another which is singular enough. "He is dead," he says,[4] "he spoke to us and now is silent, all that we touch now is his corpse." I shall not deal here with the shockingly trivial concluding sentence. But let us turn to that which precedes it: "He spoke to us and now he is silent." Let us try to take it seriously, that is, let us ignore what Sartre really meant by it, namely, that man in earlier times believed that he heard God and now is no longer capable of so believing. Let us ask whether it may not be literally true that God formerly spoke to us and is now silent, and whether this is not to be understood as the Hebrew Bible understands it, namely, that the living God is not only a self-revealing but also a self-concealing God.[5] Let us realize what it means to live in the age of such a concealment, such a divine silence, and we shall perhaps understand its implication for our existence as something entirely different from that which Sartre desires to teach us.

What Sartre desires to teach us, he says to us clearly

enough.[6] "This silence of the transcendent, combined with the perseverance of the religious need in modern man, that is the great concern to-day as yesterday. It is the problem which torments Nietzsche, Heidegger, Jaspers." In other words, existentialism must take courage, it must give up once for all the search for God, it must "forget" God.[7] After a century-long crisis of faith as well as of knowledge, man must finally recover the creative freedom which he once falsely ascribed to God. He must recognize himself as the being through whose appearance the world exists. For, says Sartre,[8] "there is no universe other than a human universe, the universe of human subjectivity." The sentence that I have just quoted sounds like the thesis of a resurrected idealism.

The problem that "torments" the existentialist thinker of our age, insofar as he does not, like Sartre, dismiss it out of hand, lies deeper than Sartre thinks. It focuses finally in the question of whether the perseverance of the "religious need" does not indicate something inherent in human existence. Does existence really mean, as Sartre thinks, existing "for oneself" encapsuled in one's own subjectivity? Or does it not essentially mean standing *over against* the x—not an x for which a certain quantity could be substituted, but rather the X itself, the undefinable and unfathomable? "God," says Sartre,[9] "is the quintessence of the Other." But the Other for Sartre[10] is he who "looks at" me, who makes me into an object, as I make him. The idea of God, moreover, he also understands as that of an inescapable witness, and if that is so, "What need have we of God? The Other is enough, no matter what other."[11] But what if God is not the quintessence of the Other, but rather its absoluteness? And what if it is not primarily the reciprocal relation of subject and object which exists between me and the other, but rather the reciprocal relation of I and Thou? Each empirical other does not, of course, remain my Thou; he becomes an It, an object for me as I for him. It is not so, however, with that absolute Other, the Absolute over against me, that undefinable and unfathomable X that I call "God." God can never become an object for me; I can attain no other relation to Him than that of the I to its eternal Thou, that of the Thou to its eternal I. But if man is no longer able to attain this relation, if God is silent toward him and he toward God, then something has taken place, not in human subjectivity but in Being itself. It would be worthier not to explain it to oneself in sensational and incompetent sayings, such as that of the "death" of God, but to endure it as it is and at the same time to move existentially toward a new happening, toward that event in which the word between heaven and earth will again be heard. Thus the perseverance of the "religious need," to which Sartre objects and which he thinks contradicts the silence of the transcendent, instead points directly to the situation in which man becomes aware of this silence as such.

Still more questionable is Sartre's demand,[12] reminiscent of Ludwig Feuerbach, that man should recover for himself the creative freedom which he ascribed to God and that he should affirm himself as the being through whom a world exists. That ordering of known phenomena which we call the world is, indeed, the composite work of a thousand human generations, but it has come into being through the fact that manifold being, which is not our work, meets us, who are, likewise, together with our subjectivity, not our work. Nor is this meeting, out of which arises the whole of the phenomena which we order into the "world," our work. All that being is *established*, we are established, our meeting with it is established, and in this way the becoming of a world, which takes place through us, is established. This establishment of a universe, including ourselves and our works, is the fundamental reality of existence which is accessible to us as living beings. Contrasted with this reality, the demand that man recover his creative freedom appears as a demagogic phrase. That "creative freedom" which really belongs to us, our participation in creation, is established, as we ourselves. It is a question of using this freedom properly, that is, in a manner worthy of the fact that it is a freedom which is given to us, nothing less and nothing more. He who sets in the place of it the postulate of the "recovery of freedom" turns aside from true human existence, which means being sent and being commissioned.

Sartre has started from the "silence" of God without asking himself what part our not hearing and our not having heard has played in that silence. From the silence he has concluded[13] that God does not exist, at any rate not for us, for a god whose object I am without his being mine does not concern me. This conclusion is possible for Sartre because he holds the subject-object relation to be the primary and exclusive relation between two beings. He does not see the original and decisive relation between I and Thou, compared with which the subject-object relation is only a classifying elaboration. Now, however, Sartre goes further[14]: One "must draw the consequences." God is silent, that is, nothing is said to one that is unconditional or unconditionally binding. "There is no sign in the world."[15] Since, therefore, no universal morality can tell us what to do, since all possibility of discovering absolute values has disappeared with God, and since man, to whom henceforth "all is permitted,"[16] is at last free, is indeed freedom itself, it is for him to determine values. "If I have done away with God the father (*si j'ai supprimé Dieu le*

père)," Sartre says literally,[17] "someone is needed to invent
values (*pour inventer les valeurs*). . . . Life has no meaning
a priori . . . it is up to you to give it a meaning, and value is
nothing else than this meaning which you choose." That is
almost exactly what Nietzsche said, and it has not become
any truer since then. One can believe in and accept a meaning or value, one can set it as a guiding light over one's life
if one has discovered it, not if one has invented it. It can be
for me an illuminating meaning, a direction-giving value only
if it has been revealed to me in my meeting with Being, not
if I have freely chosen it for myself from among the existing
possibilities and perhaps have in addition decided with some
fellow-creatures: This shall be valid from now on. The thesis
reminds me of that curious concept of Georges Sorel, the
social myth, the classic example of which is the general strike.
This avowedly unrealizable myth shall show the workers the
direction in which they shall be active, but it can function
naturally only so long as they do not read Sorel and learn
that it is just a myth.

More important than these arguments of a remarkable
psychological observer and highly gifted literary man, for
whom genuine ontological considerations are always inter-
mingled with entirely different matters, is that argument
which Heidegger, who undoubtedly belongs to the historical
rank of philosophers in the proper sense of the term, brings
forward concerning the problem of religion in our time.
These thoughts, it is true, are first explicitly expressed in the
writings of his second period, from about 1943 on, but we
already find indications of them earlier.

Like Sartre, Heidegger also starts from Nietzsche's saying
"God is dead," which he has interpreted at length.[18] It is evident to him that Nietzsche wanted in this saying to dispense

with not only God but also the absolute in all its forms, therefore, in truth, not only religion but also metaphysics. Heidegger believes that he can erect at the point of this extremest negation a new position which will be a pure ontological thinking. It is the teaching of being as attaining its illumination in or through man. In this teaching the doctrine of Parmenides which posits being as the original absolute which is prior to and above form is curiously interwoven with the Hegelian theory of the original principle which attains self-consciousness in the human spirit.

It has been possible for Heidegger to erect this new position despite the "death of God" because being for him is bound to and attains its illumination through the destiny and history of man, without its becoming thereby a function of human subjectivity. But by this it is already indicated that, to use an image that Heidegger himself avoids, God can rise from the dead. This means that the unfolding of the new ontological thought can prepare for a turning-point in which the divine, or as Heidegger, in agreement with the poet Hölderlin, prefers to say, the holy, will appear in new and still unanticipated forms. This thinking is consequently, as Heidegger repeatedly emphasizes, not atheism, for it "decides neither positively nor negatively about the possibility of God's existing."[19] Rather "through its adequate conception of existence" it makes it possible for the first time legitimately to ask "what is the ontological state of the relation of existence to the divine."

Heidegger not only protests against our regarding this view as atheism but also[20] against our regarding it as an indifferentism which must deteriorate into nihilism. He by no means wants to teach an indifference toward the religious question. The single need of this hour is, to him, much more the thinking through of the basic religious concepts, the cogitative clarification of the meaning of words such as God or the Holy. "Must we not first be able," he asks, "to understand and hear these words with the greatest care if we, as men, that is as existing beings, are to experience a relation of God to man?" But this in his opinion would belong to a new thinking of being through man. According to Heidegger's conception,[21] to be sure, it is not for man to decide whether and how the divine will reappear. Such an appearance, he explains, will take place only through the fate of being itself. Since, however, he has stated[22] as the presupposition for this appearance that "beforehand and in long preparation being itself is clarified and is experienced in its truth," there can be no doubt as to what part is to be ascribed here to human thought about truth in the determination of "whether and how the day of the holy will dawn." It is indeed precisely in human thought about truth that being becomes illuminated. Heidegger usually conceives of this still uncertain sunrise of the holy as the clear background before which "an appearance of God and the gods can begin anew."

Once[23] in interpreting Hölderlin, who had called our time an indigent one, he explains this as "the time of the gods who have fled *and* of the God who is coming." It is indigent because it stands in a double lack: "in the no longer of the departed gods and the not yet of the Coming One." As the denominating Word is wanting that could tell "who He Himself is who dwells in the holy,"[24] so is God Himself wanting. This is "the age in which God is absent";[25] the Word and God are absent together. The Word is not absent because God is absent, and God is not absent because the Word is absent. Both are absent together and appear together because of the nearness of man to being, which is at times, historically, illuminated in him. Thus, admonishes Heidegger, man living in this hour should not strive to make a God for himself, nor call any longer on an accustomed God.

Heidegger warns in this way against "religion" in general, but in particular against the prophetic principle in the Judaeo-Christian tradition. "The 'prophets' of these religions," he says,[26] "do not begin by foretelling the word of the Holy. They announce immediately the God upon whom the certainty of salvation in a supernatural blessedness reckons." Incidentally, I have never in our time encountered on a high philosophical plane such a far-reaching misunderstanding of the prophets of Israel. The prophets of Israel have never announced a God upon whom their hearers' striving for security reckoned. They have always aimed to shatter all security and to proclaim in the opened abyss of the final insecurity the unwished-for God who demands that His human creatures become real, they become human, and confounds all who imagine that they can take refuge in the certainty that the temple of God is in their midst. This is the God of the historical demand as the prophets of Israel beheld Him. The primal reality of these prophecies does not allow itself to be tossed into the attic of "religions": it is as living and actual in this historical hour as ever.

This is not the place for a critical discussion of Heidegger's theory of being. I shall only confess that for me a concept of being that means anything other than the inherent fact of all existing being, namely, that it exists, remains insurmountably empty. That is, unless I have recourse to religion and see in it a philosophical characterization of the Godhead similar to that of some Christian scholastics and mystics who contemplate, or think that they contemplate, the Godhead as it is in itself, thus as prior to creation. It should also be noted, however, that one of them, and the greatest of them all, Meister Eckhart, follows in Plato's footsteps by placing above the *esse est Deus*, as the higher truth, the sentence, "*Est enim (Deus) super esse et ens.*" Compare this with Heidegger's statement:[27] " 'Being'—that is not God and it is not a ground of the world. Being is more than all that exists and is, nonetheless, nearer than any existing thing, be it . . . an angel or God. Being is the nearest thing." If by the last sentence, however, something other is meant than that I myself am, and not indeed as the subject of a *cogito*, but as my total person, then the concept of being loses for me the character of genuine conceivability that obviously it eminently possesses for Heidegger.

I shall, however, limit myself to his theses about the divine. These theses, out of the extremest consciousness of self-drawn boundaries, are only concerned with the "appearance" of the divine. They are concerned in particular with those presuppositions of future reappearances which pertain to human thought, human thought, that is, about being. The most surprising and questionable thing about these theses to me is the fact that they designate it or him, the possible reappearance of whom is their subject, as the divine or God. In all tongues since men first found names for the eternally nameless, those who have been named by this word have been transcendent beings. They have been beings who by their nature were not given to us as knowable objects, yet beings whom we nonetheless became aware of as entering into relation with us. They stepped into relation with us, form-changing, form-preserving, formless, and allowed us to enter into relation with them. Being turned toward us, descended to us, showed itself to us, spoke to us in the immanence. The Coming One came of his own will out of the mystery of his withdrawnness; we did not cause him to come.

That has always distinguished religion from magic; for he whom man imagined that he had conjured up could not, even if he yet figured as god, be believed in any longer as god. He had become for man a bundle of powers of which man's mysterious knowledge and might could dispose. He who conjured was no longer addressed nor was any answer any longer awakened in him, and even though he recited a prayer, he no longer prayed. And indeed, as Heidegger once said[28] in interpreting the words of Hölderlin, who understood poetry as the combined work of the inspiring gods and the men inspired by them, not only does man need god, but also "the heavenly need the mortal." God needs man independent —man has divined that from of old—as partner in dialogue, as comrade in work, as one who loves Him; God needs His creature thus or wills to need him thus.

In no sphere or time in the history of the relations between the divine and the human, however, has that proved true which Heidegger further asserts, namely, that "neither men nor the gods can ever of themselves bring about the direct relation to the holy." Always, again and again, men are accosted by One who of Himself disconcerts and enraptures them, and, although overcome, the worshipper prays of himself to Him. God does not let Himself be conjured, but He also will not compel. He is of Himself, and He allows that which exists to be of itself. Both of these facts distinguish divine from demonic powers. It may not be, indeed, unimportant to God whether man gives himself or denies himself to Him. Through this giving or denying, man, the whole man with the decision of his whole being, may have an immeasurable part in the actual revelation or hiddenness of the divine. But there is no place between heaven and earth for an influence of concept-clarifying thought. He whose appearance can be effected or co-effected through such a modern magical influence clearly has only the name in common with Him whom we men, basically in agreement despite all the differences in our religious teachings, address as God. To talk of a reappearance of this conjured god of thought is inadmissable.

It is not that Heidegger is not somewhat aware of what is at stake here. Once in 1936, again in a Hölderlin interpretation, he came remarkably close to the essential reality to which I have just pointed. Hölderlin says of us humans,

> Since we exist as talk
> And can hear from one another.

Heidegger explains this thus,[29] "The gods can only enter the Word if they themselves address us and place their demand upon us. The Word that names the gods is always an answer to this demand." That is a testimony to that which I call the dialogical principle, to the dialogical relation between a divine and a human spontaneity.

But since then we have not heard the like from Heidegger. In fact, if we set next to each other all of his later statements about the divine, it appears to us as if pregnant seeds have been destroyed by a force which has passed over them. Heidegger no longer shows himself as concerned with that which there is in common between the great God-impressions of mankind and the "Coming One." Rather he summons all of the power of his thoughts and words in order to distinguish him, the "Coming One," from all that has been. To one who observes the way in which Heidegger now speaks of the historical, there can be no doubt that it is current history which has pulled up those seeds and planted in their place a belief in the entirely new. How this has gradually come about can be clearly seen if one compares with one another the occasional utterances of different stages, e.g., the Rectoral address of May, 1933, with a manifesto to the students of November 3 of the same year. In the first,[30] Heidegger praises in general terms "the glory and the greatness" of the successful "insurrection" ("*Aufbruch*"). In the second,[31] the sinister leading personality of the then current history is proclaimed as "the present and future German reality and its law." Here history no longer stands, as in all believing times, under divine judgment, but it itself, the unappealable, assigns to the Coming One his way.

Heidegger, of course, understands by history something other than a list of dated events. "History," he said in 1939,[32] "is rare." And he explained: "History exists only when the essence of truth is originally decided." But it is just his hour which he believes to be history, the very same hour whose problematics in its most inhuman manifestation led him astray. He has allied his thought, the thought of being,[33] in which he takes part and to which he ascribes the power to make ready for the rise of the holy, to that hour which he has affirmed as history. He has bound his thought to his hour as no other philosopher has done. Can he, the existential thinker, despite all this, existentially wrestle, in opposition to the hour, for a freedom devoted to the eternal and gain it? Or must he succumb to the fate of the hour, and with it also to a "holy" to which no human holiness, no hallowed standing fast of man in the face of historical delusion, responsibly answers? The questions that I ask are not rhetorical; they are true questions.

Of the two who have taken up Nietzsche's expression of the death of God, one, Sartre, has brought it and himself *ad absurdum* through his postulate of the free invention of meaning and value. The other, Heidegger, creates a concept of a rebirth of God out of the thought of truth which falls into the enticing nets of historical time. The path of this existentialism seems to vanish.

2

In contrast to Heidegger and Sartre, Jung, the leading psychologist of our day, has made religion in its historical and biographical forms the subject of comprehensive observations. He is not to be blamed for including among these observations an abundance of phenomena which I must characterize as pseudo-religious. I characterize them so because they do not bear witness to an essential personal relation to One who is experienced or believed in as being absolutely over against one. Jung properly explains he does not wish to overstep the self-drawn boundaries of psychology. This psychology offers no criterion for a qualitative distinction between the two realms, the religious and the pseudo-religious, even as little as, say, sociology as Max Weber understood it enabled him to make a distinction in kind between the charisma of Moses and that of Hitler. What Jung is to be criticized for instead is that he oversteps with sovereign license the boundaries of psychology in its most essential point. For the most part, however, he does not note it and still less account for it.

There is certainly no lack in Jung of exact psychological statements concerning religious subjects. Many times these are even accompanied by explicit emphasis on the limited validity of the statement. An example is when[34] revelation, as "the disclosure of the depths of the human soul," is termed "to begin with a psychological mode . . . from which, of course, nothing is to be concluded about what it may otherwise be." Occasionally, moreover, he declares[35] on principle that "any statement about the transcendent" shall "be avoided," for such a statement is "always only a ridiculous presumption of the human mind which is unconscious of its boundaries." If God is called a state of the soul, that is "only a statement about the knowable and not about the unknowable, about which [here the formula which has just been cited is repeated word for word] simply nothing is to be concluded." Such sentences express the legitimate position of psychology, which is authorized, like every science, to make objectively based assertions so long as in doing so it takes care not to overstep its boundaries.

They have already been overstepped if it is said[36] of religion that it is "a living relation to psychical events which do not depend upon consciousness but instead take place on the other side of it in the darkness of the psychical hinterland." This definition of religion is stated without qualification. Nor will it tolerate any. For if religion is a relation to psychic events, which cannot mean anything other than to events of one's own soul, then it is implied by this that it is not a relation to a Being or Reality which, no matter how fully it may from time to time descend to the human soul, always remains transcendent to it. More precisely, it is not the relation of an I to a Thou. This is, however, the way in which the unmistakably religious of all ages have understood their religion even if they longed most intensely to let their I be mystically absorbed into that Thou.

But religion is for all that only a matter of the human relation to God, not of God Himself. Consequently, it is more important for us to hear what Jung thinks of God Himself. He conceives of Him in general[37] as an "autonomous psychic content." This means he conceives of God not as a Being or Reality to which a psychical content corresponds, but rather as this content itself. If this is not so, he adds, "then God is indeed not real, for then He nowhere impinges upon our lives." According to this all that which is not an autonomous psychical content but instead produces or co-produces in us a psychical content is to be understood as not impinging upon our life and hence as also not real.

Despite this Jung also recognizes[38] a "reciprocal and indispensable relation between man and God." Jung immediately observes, to be sure, that God is "for our psychology . . . a function of the unconscious." However, this thesis is by no means intended to be valid only inside the boundaries of psychology, for it is opposed to the "orthodox conception" according to which God "exists for Himself," which means psychologically "that one is unaware of the fact that the action arises from one's own inner self."

It is thus unequivocally declared here that what the believer ascribes to God has its origin in his own soul. How this assertion is to be reconciled with Jung's assurance[39] that he means by all this "approximately the same thing Kant meant when he called the thing in itself a 'purely negative, borderline concept' " is to me incomprehensible. Kant has explained that the things in themselves are not to be recognized through any categories because they are not phenomena, but are only to be conceived of as an unknown something. However, that that phenomenon, for example, which I call the tree before my window originates not in my meeting with an unknown something but in my own inner self Kant simply did not mean.

In contradiction to his assertion that he wishes to avoid every statement about the transcendent, Jung identifies himself[40] with a view "according to which God does not exist 'absolutely,' that is, independent of the human subject and beyond all human conditions." This means, in effect, that the possibility is not left open that God—who, if the singular and exclusive word "God" is not to lose all meaning, cannot be limited to a single mode of existence as if it were only a question of one among many gods—exists independent of as well as related to the human subject. It is instead made clear that He does *not* exist apart from man. This is indeed a statement about the transcendent. It is a statement about what it is not and just through this about what it is. Jung's statements about the "relativity" of the divine are not psychological but metaphysical assertions, however vigorously he emphasizes "his contentment with the psychically experienceable and rejection of the metaphysical."[41]

Jung could cite in opposition to this a statement he once[42] made. "Metaphysical statements are expressions of the soul, and consequently they are psychological." However, all statements, if they are considered not according to the meaning and intention of their contents but according to the process of their psychic origin, could be described as "expressions of the soul." If, consequently, that sentence is to be taken seriously, the boundaries of psychology are forthwith abolished. These are the same boundaries that Jung says in still another place[43] that psychology must guard against "overstepping through metaphysical statements or other professions of faith." In the greatest possible contradiction to this, psychology becomes here the only admissable metaphysic. It is supposed to remain at the same time an empirical science. But it cannot be both at once.

Jung also supplies the idea of the soul which belongs to this conception. "It is the soul," he says,[44] "that produces the metaphysical expression out of inborn divine creative power; it 'sets' the distinctions between metaphysical essences. It is not only the condition for metaphysical reality, it is that reality itself." The term "sets" is not chosen without reason; what is here set forth is in fact a translation of post-Kantian idealism into psychology.[45] But that which has its place within metaphysical thinking when it is a product of philosophical reflection such as Fichte's I, can demand no such place when it is applied to the concrete individual soul or, more precisely, to the psychic in an existing human person. Nor can Jung indeed mean anything other than this. According to his explanation,[46] even the collective unconscious, the sphere of the archetypes, can enter ever again into experience only through the individual psyche, which has inherited these "typical attitudinal figures."

The real soul has without question producing powers in which primal energies of the human race have individually concentrated. "Inborn divine creative powers" seems to me, to be sure, an all too lofty and all too imprecise designation for them. This soul, however, can never legitimately make an assertion, even a metaphysical one, out of its own creative power. It can make an assertion only out of a binding real relationship to a truth which it articulates. The insight into this truth cogitatively grows in this soul out of what happens to it and what is given it to experience. Anything other than this is no real assertion but merely literary phraseology or questionable combination.

The real individual soul can never be regarded as "the metaphysically real." Its essential life, whether it admits it or not, consists of real meetings with other realities, be they other real souls or whatever else. Otherwise, one would be obliged to conceive of souls as Leibnizian monads. The ideal consequences of this conception, in particular God's eternal interference, Jung would undoubtedly be most unwilling to draw. Or the empirical real realm of individual souls, that province given over to psychology, should indeed be overstepped and a collective being called "soul" or "the soul," which only reveals itself in the individual soul and is thus transcendent, admitted. Such a metaphysical "setting" would then necessitate an adequate philosophical determining and foundation such as, to my knowledge, we nowhere find in Jung, even in the lecture on the spirit of psychology which specifically deals with the conception of the soul.

The decisive significance which this indistinct conception of the soul has for Jung's essential attitude toward religion becomes evident in the following two sentences[47] which have a common subject. "Modern consciousness, in contrast to the nineteenth century, turns with its most intimate and intense expectations to the soul." "Modern consciousness abhors faith and also as a result the religions that are founded on it." Despite his early protest that one can find in his teaching no "barbs . . . against faith or trust in higher powers,"[48] it is evident to any careful reader[49] that Jung identifies himself with the modern consciousness that "abhors" faith. According to Jung, this modern consciousness now turns itself with its "most intimate and intense expectations" to the soul. This cannot mean anything other than that it will have nothing more to do with the God believed in by religions, who is to be sure present to the soul, who reveals Himself to it, communicates with it, but remains transcendent to it in His being. Modern consciousness turns instead toward the soul as the only sphere which man can expect to harbour a divine. In short, although the new psychology protests[50] that it is "no world-view but a science," it no longer contents itself with the rôle of an interpreter of religion. It proclaims the new religion, the only one which can still be true, the religion of pure psychic immanence.

Jung speaks once,[51] and with right, of Freud's inability to understand religious experience. He himself concludes his wanderings through the grounds and abysses of religious experience, in which he has accomplished astounding feats, far outstripping all previous psychology, with the discovery that that which experiences the religious, the soul, experiences simply itself. Mystics of all ages, upon whom in fact Jung also rests his position, have proclaimed something similar; yet there are two distinctions which must be kept in mind. First, they meant by the soul which has this experience only that soul which has detached itself from all earthly bustle, from the contradictoriness of creaturely existence, and is therefore capable of apprehending the divine which is above contradictions and of letting the divine work in it. Second, they understood the experience as the oneness and becoming one of the soul with the self-contained God who, in order to enter into the reality of the world, "is born" ever again in the soul.

In the place of that detachment of the whole man from the bustle of life, Jung sets the process of "individuation," determined by a detachment of the *consciousness*. In the place of that becoming one with the Self-contained, he sets the "Self," which is also, as is well known, an originally mystical concept. In Jung, however, it is no longer a genuinely mystical concept but is transformed instead into a Gnostic one. Jung himself expresses this turning toward the Gnostic. The statement quoted above that modern consciousness turns itself to the soul is followed by the explication, "and this . . . in the Gnostic sense." We have here, if only in the form of a mere allusion, the mature expression of a tendency characteristic of Jung from the beginning of his intellectual life. In a very early writing, which was printed but was not sold to the public, it appears in direct religious language as the profession of an eminent Gnostic god, in whom good and evil are bound together and, so to speak, balance each other. This union of opposites in an all-embracing total form runs since then throughout Jung's thought. It is also of essential significance for our consideration of his teaching of individuation and the self.

Jung has given a most precise expression to that which is in question here in one of his mandala-analyses. Mandalas, as Jung has found them, not only in different religious cultures, especially those of the Orient and of the early Christian Middle Ages, but also in the drawings of neurotics and the mentally disturbed, are circular symbolic images. He understands them as representations, arising in the collective unconscious, of a wholeness and completeness which is as such a unification of opposites. They are supposed to be "unifying symbols" which include the feminine as well as the masculine, evil as well as good in their self-contained unity. Their centre, the seat of the Godhead according to Jung's interpretation, is in general, he says, especially accentuated.

There are supposed to exist, however, a few ancient mandalas and many modern ones in whose centre "no trace of divinity is to be found."[52] The symbol which takes its place in the modern images is understood by the creators of these mandalas, according to Jung, as "a centre within themselves." "The place of the deity," Jung explains, "appears to be taken by the wholeness of man." This central wholeness, which symbolizes the divine, Jung, in agreement with ancient Indian teaching, calls the self. This does not mean, says Jung, that the self takes the place of the Godhead in these images in which the unconscious of modern man expresses itself. One would grasp Jung's idea better if one said that from now on the Godhead no longer takes the place of the human self as it did in mankind up till now. Man now draws back the projection of his self on a God outside of him without thereby wishing to deify himself (as Jung here emphasizes, in contrast to another passage, in which, as we shall see, deification is clearly stated as a goal). Man does not deny a transcendent God; he simply dispenses with Him. He no longer knows the Unrecognizable; he no longer needs to pretend to know Him. In His place he knows the soul or rather the self. It is indeed not a god that "modern consciousness" abhors, but faith. Whatever may be the case concerning God, the important thing for the man of modern consciousness is to stand in no further relation of faith to Him.

This man of "modern consciousness" is not, to be sure, to be identified with the human race that is living to-day. "Mankind," says Jung,[53] "is still in the main in a psychological state of infancy—a level which cannot be leaped over." This is illustrated by the Paulinian overcoming of the law which falls only to those persons who know to set the soul in the place of conscience. This is something very few are capable of doing.

What does this mean? By conscience one understands of old, whether one ascribes to it a divine or a social origin or simply regards it as belonging to man as man, that court within the soul which concerns itself with the distinction between the right and the wrong in that which has been done and is to be done and proceeds against that which has been determined as wrong. This is not, of course, simply a question of upholding a traditional law, whether of divine or social origin. Each one who knows himself, for example, as called to a work which he has not done, each one who has not fulfilled a task which he knows to be his own, each who did not remain faithful to his vocation which he had become certain of—each such person knows what it means to say that "his conscience smites him." And in Jung himself we find[54] an excellent explication of that which we call "vocation." "Who has vocation (*Bestimmung*) hears the voice (*Stimme*) of the inner man." By this Jung means,[55] it is true, a voice which brings near to us just that which appears to be evil and to which, in his opinion, it is necessary to succumb "in part." I think, however, that he who has vocation hears at times an inner voice of an entirely different kind. This is just the voice of conscience, which compares that which he is with that which he was called to become. In clear distinction from Jung, moreover, I hold that each man in some measure has been called to something, which, to be sure, he in general successfully avoids.

But now, once again, what does it mean to set the soul in the place of the direction-giving and direction-preserving, the litigating and judging conscience? In the context of Jung's thought it cannot be understood in any other way than "in the Gnostic sense." The soul which is integrated in the Self as the unification in an all-encompassing wholeness of the opposites, especially of the opposites good and evil, dispenses with the conscience as the court which distinguishes and decides between the right and the wrong. It itself arbitrates an adjustment between the principles or effects the preservation of accord between them or their balancing out or whatever one may call it. This "way," which Jung certainly correctly qualifies[56] as "narrow as a knife-edge," has not been described and obviously is not suitable to description. The question about it leads to the question about the positive function of evil.

Jung speaks somewhat more clearly in another place[57] of the condition necessary for "the birth of the 'pneumatic man.'" It is "liberation from those desires, ambitions and passions, which imprison us in the visible world," through "intelligent fulfilment of instinctive demands"; for "he who lives his instincts can also separate himself from them." The Taoist book that Jung interprets in this way does not contain this teaching; it is well known to us from certain Gnostic circles.[58]

The "process of development proper to the psyche" which Jung calls individuation leads through the integration in the consciousness of the personal and above all the collective, or archetypal, contents of the unconscious to the realization of a "new complete form" which, as has been said, he calls the self. Here a pause for clarification is necessary. Jung wishes[59] to see the self understood as "both that or those others and the I" and individuation as a process which "does not exclude, but rather includes the world." It is necessary to grasp exactly in what sense this holds good and in what it does not. In the personality structure which arises out of the "relatively rare occurrence"[60] of the development discussed by Jung, "the others" are indeed included. However, they are included only as contents of the individual soul that shall, just as an individual soul, attain its perfection through individuation.

The actual other who meets me meets me in such a way that my soul comes in contact with his as with something that it is not and that it cannot become. My soul does not and cannot include the other, and yet can nonetheless approach the other in this most real contact. This other, what is more, is and remains over against the self, no matter what completeness the self may attain, as the other. So the self, even if it has integrated all of its unconscious elements, remains this single self, confined within itself. All beings existing over against me who become "included" in my self are possessed by it in this inclusion as an It. Only then when, having become aware of the unincludable otherness of a being, I renounce all claim to incorporating it in any way within me or making it a part of my soul, does it truly become Thou for me. This holds good for God as for man.

This is certainly not a way which leads to the goal which Jung calls the self; but it is just as little a way to the removal of self. It simply leads to a genuine contact with the existing being who meets me, to full and direct reciprocity with him. It leads from the soul which places reality in itself to the soul which enters reality.

Jung thinks that his concept of the self is also found in Meister Eckhart. This is an error. Eckhart's teaching about the soul is based on the certainty of his belief that the soul is, to be sure, like God in freedom, but that it is created while He is uncreated.[61] This essential distinction underlies all that Eckhart has to say of the relationship and nearness between God and the soul.

Jung conceives of the self which is the goal of the process of individuation as the "bridal unification of opposite halves"[62] in the soul. This means above all, as has been said, the "integration of evil,"[63] without which there can be no wholeness in the sense of this teaching. Individuation thereby realizes the complete archetype of the self, in contrast to which it is divided in the Christian symbolic into Christ and the Antichrist, representing its light and its dark aspects. In

the self the two aspects are united. The self is thus a pure
totality and as such "indistinguishable from a divine image";
self-realization is indeed to be described as "the incarnation
of God." This god who unites good and evil in himself, whose
opposites-nature also expresses itself in his male-femaleness,[64]
is a Gnostic figure, which probably is to be traced back
ultimately to the ancient Iranian divinity Zurvan (not mentioned, so far as I know, among Jung's numerous references to
the history of religions) as that out of which the light god and
his dark counterpart arose.

From the standpoint of this basic Gnostic view Jung recasts
the Jewish and Christian conception of God. In the Old Testament the Satan, the "Hinderer," is only a serving element of
God. God allows Himself to be represented by Satan, particularly for the purpose of "temptation," that is, in order to
actualize man's uttermost power of decision through affliction
and despair. Out of this God of the Old Testament Jung
makes a demiurge who is himself half-Satanic. This god then
for the sake of his "guilt," the miscarried creation of the
world (I now quote literally from Jung's speech of 1940,[65]
the like of which is nowhere to be found in the Gnostic
literature to which he refers), "must be subject to ritual
killing." By this Jung means the crucifixion of Christ. The
Trinity, moreover, is enlarged to a Quaternity in which the
autonomous devil is included as "the fourth."[66]

These, to be sure, are all, as Jung emphasizes,[67] "projections
of psychic events," "human spiritual products to which one
may not arrogate any metaphysical validity." The self seems
to him the prototype of all monotheistic systems, which are
here unmasked as hidden Gnosis. But, on the other hand, he
sees it at the same time as the *imago Dei in homine*. The soul

must indeed, he says once[68] in a formulation which so far as I know is without analogy in his other statements, have within it something which corresponds to the being of God. In any case, the self, the bridal unification of good and evil, is elevated by him to the throne of the world as the new "Incarnation." "If we should like to know," he says, "what happens in the case in which the idea of God is no longer projected as an autonomous essence, then this is the answer of the unconscious soul: the unconscious creates the idea of a deified or divine man."[69] This figure, which embraces Christ and Satan within himself,[70] is the final form of that Gnostic god, descended to earth as the realization of the "identity of God and man,"[71] which Jung once professed. He has remained faithful to this god, repeatedly intimating its prospective appearance.[72]

Jung's psychology of religion is to be understood as the announcement of that god as the Coming One. To Nietzsche's saying, "All the gods are dead, now we desire that the superman live!" Heidegger, in a note otherwise foreign to him, adds this warning[73]: "Man can never set himself in the place of God because the essence of man does not reach to God's sphere of being. On the contrary, indeed, in proportion with this impossibility, something far more uncanny may happen, the nature of which we have still hardly begun to consider. The place which, metaphysically speaking, belongs to God is the place in which the production and preservation as created being of that which exists is effected. This place of God can remain empty. Instead of it another, that is, a metaphysically corresponding place can appear, which is neither identical with God's sphere of being nor with that of man, but which, on the other hand, man can, in an eminent relation, attain. The superman does not and never will step into the place of God; the place rather in which the will to the superman arrives is another sphere in another foundation of existing things in another being." The words compel one to listen with attention. One must judge whether that which is said or intimated in them does not hold true to-day and here.

VI

Religion and Ethics

W E GRASP an essential element of the path of the human spirit known to history if we regard it from the standpoint of the changes in the relationship between the ethical and the religious. But we must consider each, both the ethical and the religious, not in one or another of its manifestations, but in its basic form.

We mean by the ethical in this strict sense the yes and no which man gives to the conduct and actions possible to him, the radical distinction between them which affirms or denies them not according to their usefulness or harmfulness for individuals and society, but according to their intrinsic value and disvalue. We find the ethical in its purity only there where the human person confronts himself with his own potentiality and distinguishes and decides in this confrontation without asking anything other than what is right and what is wrong in this his own situation. The criterion by which this distinction and decision is made may be a traditional one, or it may be one perceived by or revealed to the individual himself. What is important is that the critical flame shoot up ever again out of the depths, first illuminating, then burning and purifying. The truest source of this is a fundamental awareness inherent in all men, though in the most varied strengths and degrees of consciousness, and for the most part stifled by them. It is the individual's awareness of what he is "in truth," of what in his unique and non-repeatable created existence he is intended to be. From this awareness, when it is fully present, the comparison between what one actually is and what one is intended to be can emerge. What is found is measured against the image, no so-called ideal image, nor anything imagined by man, but an image arising out of that mystery of being itself that we call the person. Thus the genius bearing his name confronts the demonic fullness of the possible conduct and actions given to the individual in this moment. One may call the distinction and decision which arises from these depths the action of the *pre-conscience*.

We mean by the religious in this strict sense, on the other hand, the relation of the human person to the Absolute, when and insofar as the person enters and remains in this relation as a whole being. This presupposes the existence of a Being who, though in Himself unlimited and unconditioned, lets other beings, limited and conditioned indeed, exist outside Himself. He even allows them to enter into a relation with Him such as seemingly can only exist between limited and conditioned beings. Thus in my definition of the religious "the Absolute" does not mean something that the human person holds it to be, without anything being said about its existence, but the absolute reality itself, whatever the form in which it presents itself to the human person at this moment. In the reality of the religious relation the Absolute becomes in most cases personal, at times admittedly, as in the Buddhism which arose out of a personal relation to the "Unoriginated," only gradually and, as it were, reluctantly in the course of the development of a religion. It is indeed legitimate to speak of the person of God within the religious relation and in its language; but in so doing we are making no statement about the Absolute which reduces it to the personal. We are rather saying that it enters into the relationship as the Absolute

Person whom we call God. One may understand the personality of God as His act. It is, indeed, even permissible for the believer to believe that God became a person for love of him, because in our human mode of existence the only reciprocal relation with us that exists is a personal one.

We cannot, on the other hand, speak of the religious in the strict sense meant here where there is no relation and cannot be one. This is the case when a man means by his concept of God simply all that is, outside of which he himself can no longer in any way exist as a separate being who is able as such to enter into relationship with God, even though it be to lose himself ever anew in it. But this is also the case when a man means by the concept of God his own self, no matter under what complicated disguises he hides his meaning. What happens here in the pseudo-mystical chamber of ghosts and mirrors has nothing to do with the real relation or even with the real self. The real self appears only when it enters into relation with the Other. Where this relation is rejected, the real self withers away—an event which at times, indeed, can evoke most phosphorescent effects.

We must hold fast to these insights when we consider the path of the human spirit from the standpoint of the changes in the relationship between the ethical and the religious.

2

The essence of the relationship between the ethical and the religious cannot be determined by comparing the teachings of ethics and religion. One must rather penetrate into that area within each sphere where they become solidified in a concrete, personal situation. Thus it is the factual moral decision of the individual on the one hand and his factual relationship to the Absolute on the other that concerns us. In both cases it is not a mere faculty of the person that is involved, whether it be his thought or his feeling or his will, but the totality of these faculties, and more than that, the whole man. A third sphere overlying these two is not given us; we can only let the two confront each other, and in such a way that in this meeting each of them determines its relationship to the other. If from the point of view of the religious we look in such concreteness at the relation between the two spheres, we shall see its strong tendency to send forth its rays into the whole life of the person, effecting a comprehensive structural change. Living religiousness wishes to bring forth living ethos. Something essentially different meets our view if we seek to examine the connection between the two fields from the standpoint of the ethical. The man who seeks distinction and decision in his own soul cannot draw from it, from his soul, absoluteness for his scale of values. Only out of a personal relationship with the Absolute can the absoluteness of the ethical co-ordinates arise without which there is no complete awareness of self. Even when the individual calls an absolute criterion handed down by religious tradition his own, it must be reforged in the fire of the truth of his personal essential relation to the Absolute if it is to win true validity. But always it is the religious which bestows, the ethical which receives.

It would be a fundamental misunderstanding of what I am saying if one assumed that I am upholding so-called moral heteronomy or external moral laws in opposition to so-called moral autonomy or self-imposed moral laws. Where the Absolute speaks in the reciprocal relationship, there are no longer such alternatives. The whole meaning of reciprocity, indeed, lies in just this, that it does not wish to impose itself but to be freely apprehended. It gives us something to apprehend, but it does not give us the apprehension. Our act must be entirely our own for that which is to be disclosed to us to be disclosed, even that which must disclose each individual to himself. In theonomy the divine law seeks for your own, and true revelation reveals to you yourself.

3

From this point, from the reality of the relationship between the spheres in the life of the person, and only from this point can their relationship in the history of man be adequately grasped.

Twice in the history of mankind—insofar as it can be surveyed and understood by man—there has been an attempt to bind the radical distinction between good and evil to the Absolute. The two manifestations of this great enterprise of the spirit are, to be sure, as different as possible in their nature and course of development.

The first manifestation appeared in Oriental and Greek antiquity. It is the teaching of a universal continuity of meaning, whose principle appears in China as Tao, in India as Ríta, in Iran as Urta (usually pronounced Asha), and in Greece as Dike. Heavenly powers, we are told, have entrusted to man the pattern of right behaviour. But this is not an order that they have devised for man; it is their own order. Heaven does not wish to establish a special order for earth; it wishes to let it partake in its own order. The moral order is identical with the cosmic. The totality of existing beings is by its nature *one* society with *one* code of laws. It is immaterial whether the ancestors are themselves represented as gods or whether a relationship of give-and-take exists between the ancestors and the gods. In accordance with their sense and destiny, men and gods form, in the final analysis, a single

society with a single order, and it is an order of righteousness.
Men may, indeed, seek to evade it, as not infrequently even
the gods of myth do, yet the power of this order rules over
all and ultimately determines the coherence of events. The
Rita, which in the world of our perceptions distinguishes and
decides between good and evil, between the right and the
wrong, is a cosmic, but also a metacosmic, ethos of Being.
Thus the gods are addressed in a Vedic hymn: "Your Rita,
which is hidden behind the Rita [the Rita which can be
perceived in empirical life], stands eternally fast, there, where
the horses of the sun are unyoked." According to an early
Zoroastrian text, the highest god, who created the material
world, is also the father of the effective good disposition,
and of the devotion that does good works. "Heaven and
Earth," says the Chinese *Book of Transformations*, the kernel
of which is very old, "move in devotion; hence neither sun
nor moon steps out of its course." Heraclitus of Ephesus says
essentially the same thing in different form. "The sun shall
not step out of its course; else, the Erinyes, the helpers of
Dike, will find him out." The avengers of human guilt also
watch over the "holy order of the world." As a law of the
universe it was formulated even before Heraclitus by Anaximander of Miletos—"All beings must atone and do justice to
one another for the wrong they have done." And from the
school of Confucius we hear, "He who accepts responsibility
before the Tao of heaven and earth is called a man." All these
sayings complete one another as if they stood together in one
book.

4

The crisis in this doctrine common to the great cultures of
the Orient, including the Greek societies of Asia Minor, broke

out on European soil, in Greece. The philosophical expression
of this crisis is known by the name of Sophistry. Its most
characteristic criticism attacks the connection between the
ethical and the absolute by calling in question, from the
standpoint of biological facts, the cosmos as a unified pattern.
The heavenly bodies may indeed appear to us to be in that
perfect agreement which a chorus of Aeschylus calls "the
harmony of Zeus"; but where life is, another law rules, according to which the strong dispose of the weak. A few
Sophists, the radically individualistic among them, conclude
from this that the right of the strong is valid even within
human society, but most of them defend the law of society,
which unites the weak into a powerful body. Human society
determines what is good and just; it does so on the basis of
what is useful to it. Rather, since not one single society but
many and varied societies exist, one should say that societies
behave thus. The good is therefore not one and consistent, it
is "variegated and manifold." In other words, there are only
changing customs and manners, values and regulations; there
is no primordial function of assent and dissent, inherent in
Being itself, which underlies all this variety and manifoldness
and, in fact, makes it possible. "Man," sums up the greatest of
the Sophists, "is the measure of all things."

It is as a protest against this relativizing of all values that
we must understand Plato's doctrine of Ideas. It is the great
attempt of ancient thought to restore the connection of the
ethical with the Absolute and thus allow the concrete acting
man to meet once again the primal ground of Being. In line
with this intention Plato formulated at the end of his path,
as an exact counterpart to the saying of Protagoras, the opposing statement, "God is the measure of all things." Once the
belief common to the early cultures of the Orient in a unity

of the universe representing what is right had been upset and nature had been split into a harmonious cosmos and a discordant bios, then the world of things could no longer serve man as a model and pattern. It itself must be confronted by an inviolable, archetypal world of pure Forms.

But the design leads on as if of necessity even to Plato's construction of this higher world, whose highest summit is the idea of the Good or God. The eternal Ethos itself, the ground of being of that universal human function that sets the yes against the no and pushes to a decision, becomes the highest "form" of the Absolute. It is the "Good and the Should-Be" that binds and holds together all being. With a clarity of thought never before attained, man is given here the task of realizing the unconditionality of Right through his person. The objective "imitation" of Ideas by things becomes transformed in and through the subjectivity into the spiritual act of becoming just. This positing of the ethical function as transcendental becomes possible through one of the most daring of man's thoughts. It is that the Good "towers above being in dignity and power" as the "primal cause of all that is just and beautiful." The Good brings each individual thing into being not simply that it may exist but that it may perfectly become that which it is meant to be. The distinction between the affirmed and the negated that leads to the conquest of the no by the yes stands above being still undifferentiated as such. In its innermost depths, one nears the mystery of God, for not Being, but only Perfect Being, may be called God. "If one does not cease," says Plato, "until one has reached the Good itself through knowledge itself, then one reaches the end of the knowable." But where does one recognize the Good? To this question Plato gives us no specific answer, but we remain close to him if we say that the Good is recognized there where it reveals itself to the individual who decides with his whole being to become that which he is meant to be. And in fact, whether it takes place in the soul or in the world, nothing is so mysterious as the appearance of the Good. In its light all secret teachings appear as learnable conventions; the essential relation of the human person to that which "towers above being" cannot be learned, it can only be awakened.

5

Plato's daring attempt to set a world of Ideas in the place of the collapsing prototypal heavenly world that guaranteed the absoluteness of the highest values to the great Oriental cultures did not succeed, however great and persevering its influence. The process which had begun continued, leading to the dissolution of the absoluteness of the ethical co-ordinates and, in constant interaction with it, to the disintegration of the old world.

Long before this, however, the first stage had been completed in the second great attempt in the history of the human spirit to bind the radical distinction between good and evil with the Absolute. This attempt, as I said before, was utterly different from the first in its method and course of development. It did not originate, like the first, in a connected group of higher cultures stretching over a continent. It originated in a band of cattle-breeders and occasional farmers who left the high civilization of Egypt, where, as a foreign people, they had eked out a half-free, half-slave existence, to become wanderers and land-seekers and who on the way, in an oasis, constituted themselves as a covenantal union of tribes united by their common faith in God. This "God of Israel" was a giver and protector of law, like some other Semitic tribal gods, but the covenant that was made with Him was based on such an earnest, such a genuinely demanded and protected distinction between right and wrong as had not been known in any of those tribes. The spiritual leaders ever again and ever more clearly told the people who had then arisen that He was "the Judge of the whole earth," who had now chosen just this people as His immediate following in order that it might begin to fulfil His righteousness. This righteousness, the confirmation, namely, of what is just and the overcoming of what is unjust, was here not already embodied in a heavenly society that should serve as a model for the human one. It was not the cosmic order which was decisive but its sovereign, the Lord of heaven and earth, who taught the human creature formed by His hand to distinguish in their souls between good and evil as He Himself, creating the world, had distinguished between light and darkness.

It is customary to see the connection between the ethical and the religious in Israel exclusively in the form of a heavenly command accompanied by a threat of punishment. To do this is to miss what is essential. For the giving of the law at Sinai is properly understood as the body of rules which the divine Ruler conferred upon His people in the hour of His ascension to the throne. All the prescriptions of this body of rules, both the ritual and the ethical, are intended to lead beyond themselves into the sphere of the "holy." The people's goal was set not by their being bidden to become a "good" people but a "holy" one. Thus every moral demand is set forth as one that shall raise man, the human people, to the sphere where the ethical merges into the religious, or rather where the difference between the ethical and the religious is suspended in the breathing-space of the divine. This is expressed with unsurpassable clarity in the reason given for the goal that is set. Israel shall become holy, "for I am holy." The imitation of God by man, the "following in His way," can be fulfilled naturally only in those divine attributes turned towards the human ethos, in justice and love, and all the attributes are transparent into the Holiness above the attributes, to be reproduced in the radically different human dimension. The absolute norm is given to show the way that leads before the face of the Absolute.

The presupposition for this connection between the ethical and the religious, however, is the basic view that man, while created by God, was established by Him in an independence which has since remained undiminished. In this independence he stands over against God. So man takes part with full freedom and spontaneity in the dialogue between the two which forms the essence of existence. That this is so despite God's unlimited power and knowledge is just that which constitutes the mystery of man's creation. In this is founded the lasting reality of the distinction and decision which man consummates in his soul.

The stream of Christianity, flowing over the world from the source of Israel and strengthened by mighty influxes, especially the Iranian and the Greek, arose at a time in Hellenistic civilization, and especially in its religious life, when the element of the people was being displaced by that of the individual. Christianity is "Hellenistic" insofar as it surrenders the concept of the "holy people" and recognizes only a personal holiness. Individual religiousness thus attains a hitherto unheard-of intensity and inwardness, especially since the ever-present image of Christ permits the individual a far more concrete relation of following after and imitation than does the imageless nature of the God of Israel, who is a self-revealing but not less a self-concealing (in no way, to be sure, as people are accustomed to say, a hidden) God. With this God, not fixing Himself to any form and withdrawing Himself from every manifestation, the peoples won to Christianity would certainly not have been able to enter into an unmediated relation. They did not stand, like Israel, in a fundamental relationship to Him as the people of a covenant. In connection with this Christian individualism, moreover, the relationship between the ethical and the religious was impaired. For when a sanctification of the people as a people is no longer recognized or no longer taken seriously, then the peoples accept the new faith not as peoples but as collections of individuals. Even where mass conversions take place, the people as a people remains unbaptized; it does not enter as a people into the new covenant that has been proclaimed.

This means that here a great spiritual power, such as was prophecy in Israel, no longer executes the task of denouncing and reproving, for the sake of the people's holiness, the unholy both in public life and in the private life of the individual who has been participating in this public life, so to speak, "in good conscience." Certainly in the history of Christian peoples there has been no lack of men of the spirit afire and ready for martyrdom in the struggle for righteousness; but the injunction, "You shall become a holy people unto me," no longer stood living behind them.

Something else, of still deeper import, was added to this. It too was connected with the meaningful and legitimate development of the fundamental supremacy of the religious. That which formed the kernel of the prophetic teaching in Israel was the work of life to be fulfilled out of the full intention of faith, and the intention of faith was the innermost action of man. It was against ritual works emptied of the intention of faith that the prophets fought. It was against moral works emptied of the intention of faith that their successors in the time of Jesus fought, to whom belonged the great Pharisaic teachers and Jesus himself. The Pauline and the Paulinistic theology depreciated works for the sake of faith. It left undeveloped that which bound the two together, the demand for intention of faith, intention of work out of faith, the demand which underlay the proclamation of that which is pleasing to God from the first Biblical prophets to the Sermon on the Mount. But the tendency from Augustine to the Reformation was to see faith as a gift of God. This sublime conception, with all that goes with it, resulted in the retreating into obscurity of the Israelite mystery of man as an independent partner of God. The dogma of original sin was not, indeed, adapted to further that especial connection of the ethical with the religious that true theonomy seeks to realize through the faithful autonomy of man.

In the teachings of the correspondence between heaven and earth, found in the great Asiatic cultures, the normative principle is not yet differentiated at all from the theological (theology being understood as religion's reflection on itself). There only exists a normative side of truth turned toward man. In the teaching of Israel the ethos is an inherent function of religion, no longer one side indeed but a direct effect of it. In Christianity, which gives the character of exclusiveness to the Israelite belief in the indispensable grace of God, the norm, even if it steps forth as the "new law," can no longer occupy a central place. It is thus made easy for the secular norm to gain ever more ground at its expense. In its political form, to be sure, the secular norm seeks to secure an absolute religious basis through the concept of the divine right of kings and other means. The true binding of the ethical to the Absolute, however, is here ever less present.

6

The crisis of the second great attempt to bind the ethical to the Absolute extends into our time. Like the first, it also found its intellectual expression in a philosophical movement that relativized values, though one that was, to be sure, far more differentiated than that of the Sophists. It had its prelude already in the seventeenth century in views such as that of Hobbes, which remind one in some points of the formulations of a Sophistical text of the fifth century B.C.* Its decisive development, however, takes place in the nineteenth century through an attitude of mind that one might call a philosophy of reduction or detection. He who consummated it, Nietzsche, called it "the art of mistrust."

This philosophy, which, like that of the Sophists, connects the biological perspective with the historical and the psychological, seeks to unmask the spiritual world as a system of deceptions and self-deceptions, of "ideologies" and "sublimations."

It finds its actual beginning in Feuerbach's critique of religion, which developed Protagoras' saying that man is the measure of all things in a seemingly inverse way. It is summed up in the sentence: "What man is not, but what he wills to be or wishes to be, just that and only that, nothing else, is God." A direct path leads from Feuerbach to Marx, except that for Marx a statement of this sort, being metaphysical and unhistorical, would have no real meaning. For Marx, following Vico, there is no knowledge but the historical. He transforms Feuerbach's thesis, broadening it on the one hand to include all religious, moral, political, and philosophical ideas but inserting all these on the other hand into the historical process.

* Anonymus Jamblichi.

This process, in turn, is to be understood only through the changes in the conditions of production and the conflicts that arise out of it. In every morality, he argues, the conditions of the existence of the ruling class are ideally expressed. As long as the class struggle exists, all distinction between good and evil is merely a function of it, all life-norms either expressions of power or weapons for its enforcement. This holds true essentially not only for the changing moral contents, but also for moral valuing as such.

Insofar as Nietzsche's critique of morals remains in the historical sphere, it can be understood objectively, though Nietzsche himself was, of course, far from so understanding it, as a modification of Marx's doctrine of ideologies. He too saw historical morals as the expression and instruments of the power struggle between ruling and oppressed classes, only also from the side of the latter. It is on this side, the "slave morality," which he understands Christianity to be, that he particularly fixes his attention. Underlying this conception of the historical appearance of moralities is his view of the genesis of values, according to which values and their transformations stand "in relationship to the growth of the power of the setter of values." Underlying this view, in turn, is the methaphysical conception that the life of the spirit, like all life, can be reduced to the single principle of the "will to power." But now Nietzsche executes a singular reversal. The "slave morality," which turns against the will to power, is identified with morality as a whole, as if the "master morality," of which Nietzsche approves, did not exist at all.

On the one hand, he proclaims a biologically-based morality. "I teach negation of all that weakens. I teach affirmation of all that strengthens." But on the other hand, he explains that scepticism of all morality is that which is decisive and our age is that of the decline of the moral interpretation of the world. This decline will end in nihilism, which he himself professes. This means that "the highest values lose their value" so that now a goal for existence is wanting. Nihilism shall now, however, be overcome through creating a goal "which will remain poised above mankind and above the individual." This means that a new goal, a new meaning of existence and a new value, are set by Nietzsche's teaching of the Superman. He has not noticed, to be sure, that all this is already basically abrogated through his other teaching, that of the eternal return of the same, which he himself calls "the extremest form of nihilism" and the eternalization of the meaningless.

Nietzsche knew, so basically as not many modern thinkers before him, that the absoluteness of ethical values is rooted in our relationship to the Absolute. And he understood this hour of human history as that in which "the belief in God and in an essential moral order can no longer be held." His decisive utterance is the cry "God is dead." But he could bear this proclamation only as a turning-point, not as an end-point. Time and again he seeks a conception that will show a way out that might save God for those who had become godless. "Religions are wrecked by their belief in morality," he says. "The Christian moral God is untenable." But this does not yet lead to simple atheism "as though no other kinds of gods could exist." From within man himself must come forth, if not the new god himself, at least a valid substitute for God, the "Superman." But this is at the same time the measure of the new, life-affirming values; on this concept is founded the new biological scale of values in which the values good-evil are replaced by the values strong-weak. And again Nietzsche does not notice that all the ambiguity that has ever attached itself to the values good-evil is fatally surpassed by the intrinsic ambiguity of the values strong-weak. "The Sophists," says Nietzsche, "have the courage common to all strong spirits of knowing their immorality. The Sophists were Greek; when Socrates and Plato took the part of virtue and righteousness, they were Jews or I know not what." Nietzsche himself wanted to conquer the nihilism which he himself had consummated; as a result he came to grief. This is not meant in the sense in which one could say of Plato that he came to grief because he had no success in the historical course of events. What is meant, rather, is that in contradistinction to the doctrine of Ideas, the "teaching of the Superman" is no teaching at all and that in contradistinction to the value-scale defined by the idea of the Good, the value-scale strong-weak is no value-scale at all.

The situation in which we find ourselves is partially conditioned by this abortive undertaking of nihilism both to fulfil and to overcome itself at the same time. But there is one thing that we may learn from nihilism. A purely moral structure of authority will not lead us out of this situation into a different one.

VII

On the Suspension of the Ethical

THE FIRST book of Kierkegaard's that I read as a young man was *Fear and Trembling*, which is built entirely upon the Biblical narrative of the sacrifice of Isaac. I still think of that hour to-day because it was then that I received the impulse to reflect upon the categories of the ethical and the religious in their relation to each other.

Through the example of the temptation of Abraham this book sets forth the idea that there is a "teleological suspension of the ethical," that the validity of a moral duty can be at times suspended in accordance with the purpose of something higher, of the highest. When God commands one to murder his son, the immorality of the immoral is suspended for the duration of this situation. What is more, that which is otherwise purely evil is for the duration of this situation purely good because it has become pleasing to God. In the place of the universal and the universally valid steps something which is founded exclusively in the personal relation between God and "the Single One." But just through this the ethical, the universal and the universally valid, is relativized. Its values and laws are banished from the absolute into the relative; for that which is a duty in the sphere of the ethical possesses no absoluteness as soon as it is confronted with the absolute duty toward God. "But what is duty?" asks Kierkegaard. "Duty is indeed just the expression for God's will!" In other words, God establishes the order of good and evil, and breaks through it where He wishes. He does so from person to person, that is, in direct personal relation with the individual.

On the deadly seriousness of this "from person to person" Kierkegaard has, it is true, laid the greatest possible stress. He has declared most clearly that this trial will only be laid upon one who is worthy of being called God's chosen one. "But who," he asks, "is such a one?" In particular, he assures us time and again that he himself does not have this courage of faith which is necessary to plunge confidently, with closed eyes, into the absurd. It is impossible for him to perform the paradoxical movement of faith that Abraham performed. One must keep in mind, however, the fact that Kierkegaard also states that he has fought to become "the Single One" in the strictest sense of the term but has not attained it and the fact that he nonetheless once considered having the words "that Single One" placed upon his grave. There are many indications that when he described how Abraham gave up his son and nonetheless believed that he would not lose him (so Kierkegaard understood the event), he had in mind the day, a little more than a year before, when he himself broke his engagement with his beloved and yet thought that he would be able to preserve it in a higher, incomprehensible dimension. In the way of this union (he once explained) "there stood a divine protest"* though he had, to be sure, no lasting confidence in this idea. So little confidence had he, in fact, that in the year of the publication of *Fear and Trembling* he was able to set down the sentence, "Had I had faith, I would have remained with her."

The event is here removed out of the situation between Abraham and God, in which God breaks through the ethical order which He Himself established, into a sphere where what happens takes place in a much less unequivocal fashion

* She also stated once, much later, that he had sacrificed her to God.

than in the Biblical narrative. "That which the Single One is to understand by Isaac," says Kierkegaard, "can be decided only by and for himself." That means, clearly and precisely, that he does not learn it, at least not unmistakably, from God. God demands a sacrifice of him, but it is left to the Single One to interpret what that sacrifice is. His interpretation will always be determined by his life-circumstances in this hour. How differently the Biblical voice speaks here! "Thy son, thine only one, whom thou lovest, Isaac." There is nothing here to interpret. The man who hears learns entirely what is demanded of him; the God who speaks proposes no riddles.

But we still have not arrived at the decisive problematics. This first appears to us when Kierkegaard compares his Abraham with Agamemnon, who is getting ready to sacrifice Iphigenia. Agamemnon is the tragic hero, who is called upon by "the universal" to sacrifice for the welfare of his people. He, therefore, "remains within the borders of the ethical," which Abraham, "the knight of faith," crosses over. Everything depends upon this, that Abraham crosses over them with the paradoxical movement of faith. Otherwise all becomes a demonic temptation ("*Anfechtung*"), the readiness to sacrifice a readiness to murder, and "Abraham is lost." This also is decided in "absolute isolation." "The knight of faith," says Kierkegaard, "is left to his own resources, single and alone, and therein lies the dreadful."

This is true insofar as there is no one on earth who can help him to come to a decision and to perform "the movement of infinity." But Kierkegaard here takes for granted something that cannot be taken for granted even in the world of Abraham, much less in ours. He does not take into consideration the fact that the problematics of the decision of faith is preceded by the problematics of the hearing itself. Who is it whose voice one hears? For Kierkegaard it is self-evident because of the Christian tradition in which he grew up that he who demands the sacrifice is none other than God. But for the Bible, at least for the Old Testament, it is not without further question self-evident. Indeed a certain "insti- gation" to a forbidden action is even ascribed in one place to God (2 Samuel 24:1) and in another to Satan (1 Chronicles 21:1).

Abraham, to be sure, could not confuse with another the voice which once bade him leave his homeland and which he at that time recognized as the voice of God without the speaker saying to him who he was. And God did indeed "tempt" him. Through the extremest demand He drew forth the innermost readiness to sacrifice out of the depths of Abraham's being, and He allowed this readiness to grow to the full intention to act. He thus made it possible for Abra- ham's relation to Him, God, to become wholly real. But then, when no further hindrance stood between the intention and the deed, He contented Himself with Abraham's fulfilled readiness and prevented the action.

It can happen, however, that a sinful man is uncertain whether he does not have to sacrifice his (perhaps also very beloved) son to God for his sins (Micah 6:7). For Moloch imitates the voice of God. In contrast to this, God Himself demands of this as of every man (not of Abraham, His chosen one, but of you and me) nothing more than justice and love, and that he "walk humbly" with Him, with God (Micah 6:8)—in other words, not much more than the fundamental ethical.

Where, therefore, the "suspension" of the ethical is con- cerned, the question of questions which takes precedence over every other is: Are you really addressed by the Absolute or by one of his apes? It should be noted in this connection that, according to the report of the Bible, the divine voice which speaks to the Single One is the "voice of a thin silence" (1 Kings 19:21).* The voice of Moloch, in contrast, usually prefers a mighty roaring. However, in our age especially, it appears to be extremely difficult to distinguish the one from the other.

Ours is an age in which the suspension of the ethical fills the world in a caricaturized form. The apes of the Absolute, to be sure, have always in the past bustled about on earth. Ever and ever again men are commanded from out of the darkness to sacrifice their Isaac. *Here* the sentence is valid, "That which the Single One is to understand by Isaac, can be decided only by and for himself." But stored away in men's hearts, there were in all those times images of the Absolute, partly pallid, partly crude, altogether false and yet true, fleeting as an image in a dream yet verified in eternity. Inadequate as this presence certainly was, insofar as one bore it concretely in mind one only needed to call on it in order not to succumb to the deception of the voices.

That is no longer so since, in Nietzsche's words, "God is dead," that is, realistically speaking, since the image-making power of the human heart has been in decline so that the spiritual pupil can no longer catch a glimpse of the appearance of the Absolute. False absolutes rule over the soul, which is no longer able to put them to flight through the image of the true. Everywhere, over the whole surface of the human world—in the East and in the West, from the left and from

* A bold visual metaphor for an acoustical event: It is a silence, but not a thick and solid one, rather one that is of such veil-like thinness that the Word shines through it.

the right, they pierce unhindered through the level of the ethical and demand of you "the sacrifice." Time and again, when I ask well-conditioned young souls, "Why do you give up your dearest possession, your personal integrity?" they answer me, "Even this, this most difficult sacrifice, is the thing that is needed in order that. . . ." It makes no difference, "in order that equality may come" or "in order that freedom may come," it makes no difference! And they bring the sacrifice faithfully. In the realm of Moloch honest men lie and compassionate men torture. And they really and truly believe that brother-murder will prepare the way for brother-hood! There appears to be no escape from the most evil of all idolatry.

There is no escape from it until the new conscience of men has arisen that will summon them to guard with the innermost power of their souls against the confusion of the relative with the Absolute, that will enable them to see through illusion and to recognize this confusion for what it is. To penetrate again and again into the false absolute with an incorruptible, probing glance until one has discovered its limits, its limitedness—there is to-day perhaps no other way to reawaken the power of the pupil to glimpse the never-vanishing appearance of the Absolute.

VIII

God and the Spirit of Man

THIS BOOK discusses the relations between religion and philosophy in the history of the spirit and deals with the part that philosophy has played in its late period in making God and all absoluteness appear unreal.

If philosophy is here set in contrast to religion, what is meant by religion is not the massive fulness of statements, concepts, and activities that one customarily describes by this name and that men sometimes long for more than for God. Religion is essentially the act of holding fast to God. And that does not mean holding fast to an image that one has made of God, nor even holding fast to the faith in God that one has conceived. It means holding fast to the existing God. The earth would not hold fast to its conception of the sun (if it had one) nor to its connection with it, but to the sun itself.

In contrast to religion so understood, philosophy is here regarded as the process, reaching from the early becoming independent of reflection to its more contemporary crisis, the last stage of which is the intellectual letting go of God.

This process begins with man's no longer contenting himself, as did the pre-philosophical man, with picturing the living God, to whom one formerly only called—with a call of despair or rapture which occasionally became His first name—as a Something, a thing among things, a being among beings, an It.

The beginning of philosophizing means that this Something changes from an object of imagination, wishes, and feelings to one that is conceptually comprehensible, to an object of thought. It does not matter whether this object of thought is called "Speech" (*Logos*), because in all and each one hears it speak, answer, and directly address one, or "the Unlimited" (*Apeiron*), because it has already leapt over every limit that one may try to set for it, or simply "Being," or whatever. If the living quality of the conception of God refuses to enter into this conceptual image, it is tolerated alongside of it, usually in an unprecise form, as in the end identical with it or at least essentially dependent on it. Or it is depreciated as an unsatisfactory surrogate for the help of men incapable of thought.

In the progress of its philosophizing the human spirit is ever more inclined to fuse characteristically this conception, of the Absolute as object of an adequate thought, with itself, the human spirit. In the course of this process, the idea which was at first noetically contemplated finally becomes the potentiality of the spirit itself that thinks it, and it attains on the way of the spirit its actuality. The subject, which appeared to be attached to being in order to perform for it the service of contemplation, asserts that it itself produced and produces being. Until, finally, all that is over against us, everything that accosts us and takes possession of us, all partnership of existence, is dissolved in free-floating subjectivity.

The next step already takes us to the stage familiar to us, the stage that understands itself as the final one and plays with its finality: the human spirit, which adjudges to itself mastery over its work, annihilates conceptually the absoluteness of the absolute. It may yet imagine that it, the spirit, still remains there as bearer of all things and coiner of all values; in truth, it has also destroyed its own absoluteness along with absoluteness in general. The spirit can now no longer exist as an independent essence. There now exists only a product of human individuals called spirit, a product which they contain and secrete like mucus and urine.

In this stage there first takes place the conceptual letting go of God because only now philosophy cuts off its own hands, the hands with which it was able to grasp and hold Him.

But an analogous process takes place on the other side, in the development of religion itself (in the usual broad sense of the word).

From the earliest times the reality of the relation of faith, man's standing before the face of God, world-happening as dialogue, has been threatened by the impulse to control the power yonder. Instead of understanding events as calls which make demands on one, one wishes oneself to demand without having to hearken. "I have," says man, "power over the powers I conjure." And that continues, with sundry modifications, wherever one celebrates rites without being turned to the Thou and without really meaning its Presence.

The other pseudoreligious counterpart of the relation of faith, not so elementally active as conjuration but acting with the mature power of the intellect, is unveiling. Here one takes the position of raising the veil of the manifest, which divides the revealed from the hidden, and leading forth the divine mysteries. "I am," says man, "acquainted with the unknown, and I make it known." The supposedly divine It that the magician manipulates as the technician his dynamo, the Gnostic lays bare, the whole divine apparatus. His heirs are not "theosophies" and their neighbours alone; in many theologies also, unveiling gestures are to be discovered behind the interpreting ones.

We find this replacement of I-Thou by an I-It in manifold

forms in that new philosophy of religion which seeks to "save" religion. In it the "I" of this relation steps ever more into the foreground as "subject" of "religious feeling," as profiter from a pragmatist decision to believe, and the like.

Much more important than all this, however, is an event penetrating to the innermost depth of the religious life, an event which may be described as the subjectivizing of the act of faith itself. Its essence can be grasped most clearly through the example of prayer.

We call prayer in the pregnant sense of the term that speech of man to God which, whatever else is asked, ultimately asks for the manifestation of the divine Presence, for this Presence's becoming dialogically perceivable. The single presupposition of a genuine state of prayer is thus the readiness of the whole man for this Presence, simple turned-towardness, unreserved spontaneity. This spontaneity, ascending from the roots, succeeds time and again in overcoming all that disturbs and diverts. But in this our stage of subjectivized reflection not only the concentration of the one who prays, but also his spontaneity is assailed. The assailant is consciousness, the over-consciousness of this man here that he is praying, that he is *praying*, that *he* is praying. And the assailant appears to be invincible. The subjective knowledge of the one turning-towards about his turning-towards, this holding back of an I which does not enter into the action with the rest of the person, an I to which the action is an object—all this depossesses the moment, takes away its spontaneity. The specifically modern man who has not yet let go of God knows what that means: he who is not present perceives no Presence.

One must understand this correctly: this is not a question of a special case of the known sickness of modern man, who must attend his own actions as spectator. It is the confession of the Absolute into which he brings his unfaithfulness to the Absolute, and it is the relation between the Absolute and him upon which this unfaithfulness works, in the middle of the statement of trust. And now he too who is seemingly holding fast to God becomes aware of the eclipsed Transcendence.

What is it that we mean when we speak of an eclipse of God which is even now taking place? Through this metaphor we make the tremendous assumption that we can glance up to God with our "mind's eye," or rather being's eye, as with our bodily eye to the sun; and that something can step between our existence and His as between the earth and the sun. That this glance of the being exists, wholly unillusory, yielding no images yet first making possible all images, no other court in the world attests than that of faith. It is not to be proved; it is only to be experienced; man has experienced it. And that other, that which steps in between, one also experiences, to-day. I have spoken of it since I have recognized it, and as exactly as my perception allowed me.

The double nature of man, as the being that is both brought forth from "below" and sent from "above," results in the duality of his basic characteristics. These cannot be understood through the categories of the individual man existing-for-himself, but only through the categories of his existing as man-with-man. As a being who is sent, man exists over against the existing being before which he is placed. As a being who is brought forth, he finds himself beside all existing beings in the world, beside which he is set. The first of these categories has its living reality in the relation I-Thou, the second has its reality in the relation I-It. The second always brings us only to the aspects of an existing being, not to that being itself. Even the most intimate contact with another remains covered over by an aspect if the other has not become Thou for me. Only the first relation, that which establishes essential immediacy between me and an existing being, brings me just thereby not to an aspect of it but to that being itself. To be sure, it brings me only to the existential meeting with it; it does not somehow put me in a position to view it objectively in its being. As soon as an objective viewing is established, we are given only an aspect and ever again only an aspect. But it is also only the relation I-Thou in which we can meet God at all, because of Him, in absolute contrast to all other existing beings, no objective aspect can be attained. Even a vision yields no objective viewing, and he who strains to hold fast an after-image after the cessation of the full I-Thou relation has already lost the vision.

It is not the case, however, that the I in both relations, I-Thou and I-It, is the same. Rather where and when the beings around one are seen and treated as objects of observation, reflection, use, perhaps also of solicitude or help, there and then another I is spoken, another I manifested, another I exists than where and when one stands with the whole of one's being over against another being and steps into an essential relation with him. Everyone who knows both in himself—and that is the life of man, that one comes to know both in himself and ever again both—knows whereof I speak. Both together build up human existence; it is only a question of which of the two is at any particular time the architect and which is his assistant. Rather, it is a question of whether the I-Thou relation remains the architect, for it is self-evident that it cannot be employed as assistant. If it does not command, then it is already disappearing.

In our age the I-It relation, gigantically swollen, has usurped, practically uncontested, the mastery and the rule. The I of this relation, an I that possesses all, makes all, succeeds with all, this I that is unable to say Thou, unable to meet a being essentially, is the lord of the hour. This selfhood that has become omnipotent, with all the It around it, can naturally acknowledge neither God nor any genuine absolute which manifests itself to men as of non-human origin. It steps in between and shuts off from us the light of heaven.

Such is the nature of this hour. But what of the next? It is a modern superstition that the character of an age acts as fate for the next. One lets it prescribe what is possible to do and hence what is permitted. One surely cannot swim against the stream, one says. But perhaps one can swim with a new stream whose source is still hidden? In another image, the I-Thou relation has gone into the catacombs—who can say with how much greater power it will step forth! Who can say when the I-It relation will be directed anew to its assisting place and activity!

The most important events in the history of that embodied possibility called man are the occasionally occurring beginnings of new epochs, determined by forces previously invisible or unregarded. Each age is, of course, a continuation of the preceding one, but a continuation can be confirmation and it can be refutation.

Something is taking place in the depths that as yet needs no name. To-morrow even it may happen that it will be beckoned to from the heights, across the heads of the earthly archons. The eclipse of the light of God is no extinction; even to-morrow that which has stepped in between may give way.

IX

Supplement: Reply to C. G. Jung

IN THE face of C. G. Jung's reply to my criticism of him in "Religion and Modern Thinking,"* it will be sufficient to clarify anew my position in regard to his arguments.

I have not, as he thinks, placed in question any essential part of his empirical psychiatric material. That would certainly be unauthorized. Nor have I criticized any of his psychological theses. This also is not my affair. I have merely pointed out that he makes assertions about religious subjects which overstep the realms of the psychiatric and the psychological—contrary to his assurance that he remains strictly inside them. Whether I have demonstrated this the conscientious reader can ascertain through checking my citations in their context. I have been at pains to facilitate this for him through careful statement of sources. Jung disputes my demonstration, and the method he uses to do so is made clear in his reply.

I have pointed out that Jung describes it as a "fact," "that the divine action arises from one's own inner self" and that he sets this fact in contrast to the "orthodox conception," according to which God "exists for Himself." He explains that God does not exist independent of the human subject. The controversial question is therefore this: Is God merely a psychic phenomenon or does He also exist independently

* The chapter "Religion and Modern Thinking" appeared in German in the February, 1952, issue of the periodical *Merkur*. The May issue carried an answer by Prof. C. G. Jung and my reply which follows here.

of the psyche of men? Jung answers, God does not exist for Himself. One can also state the question in this way: Does that which the man of faith calls the divine action arise merely from his own inner self or can the action of a super-psychic Being also be included in it? Jung answers that it arises from one's own inner self. I have remarked in this regard that these are not legitimate assertions of a psychologist who as such has no right to declare what exists beyond the psychic and what does not, or to what extent there are actions which come from elsewhere. But Jung now replies: "I have made judgments only about the unconscious!" He further states, "Why, I say explicitly that all, *simply all* [italics mine] that which is stated about God, is human statement, i.e. psychic." This view, strange to say, he again limits: He is of the opinion, he says, "that all statements about God proceed *first of all* [italics mine] from the soul."

Compare, to begin with, the first of these sentences with the theses of Jung which I have quoted above. To explain emphatically that the action of one of the powers of the unconscious arises from one's own inner self, or that it does not exist independent of the human subject, would be a non-sensical tautology once the terminology of the "unconscious" is laid down. It would simply mean that the psychic realm designated as the unconscious is psychic. The thesis first acquires a meaning through the fact that it reaches out with its No beyond the sphere of the powers of the unconscious and the psychic sphere in general. Jung now, to be sure, denies that it has this meaning. And he refers in this connec-tion to the fact that all statements about God are "human statements, i.e. psychic." This sentence deserves a closer examination.

I see no possibility certainly of conducting a discussion

otherwise than on the ground of this presupposition. (As a rule, I do not bring my own beliefs into the discussion but hold them in check for the sake of human conversation. But it must be mentioned here for the sake of full clarity that my own belief in revelation, which is not mixed up with any "orthodoxy," does not mean that I believe that finished statements about God were handed down from heaven to earth. Rather it means that the human substance is melted by the spiritual fire which visits it, and there now breaks forth from it a word, a statement, which is human in its meaning and form, human conception and human speech, and yet witnesses to Him who stimulated it and to His will. We are revealed to ourselves—and cannot express it otherwise than as something revealed.) Not only statements about God, but all statements in general are "human." Yet is anything positive or negative thereby ascertained about their truth? The distinction which is here in question is thus not that between psychic and non-psychic statements, but that between psychic statements to which a super-psychic reality corresponds and psychic statements to which none corresponds. The science of psychology, however, is not authorized to make such a distinction; it presumes too much, it injures itself, if it does so. The only activity that properly belongs to the science of psychology in this connection is a reasoned restraint. Jung does not exercise such a restraint when he explains that God cannot exist independent of men. For, once again, if this is a statement about an archetype called God, then the emphatic assurance that it is a psychic factor is certainly unnecessary (What else could it be?). But if it is a statement about some extra-psychical Being which corresponds to this psychic factor, namely the statement that no such Being exists, then we have here, instead of the indicated restraint, an illicit

overstepping of boundaries. We should at last extricate ourselves from this ingenious ambiguity!

But Jung now brings to my attention that men do in fact
have many and different images of God, which they themselves make. I think I was already aware of this and have
many times stated and explained it. But that which is essential
is still the fact that they are just images. No man of faith
imagines that he possesses a photograph of God or a reflection
of God in a magic mirror. Each knows that he has painted it,
he and others. But it was painted just as an image, a likeness.
That means it was painted in the intention of faith directed
towards the Imageless whom the image "portrays," that is,
means. This intention of faith directed towards an existing
Being, towards One Who exists, is common to men who
believe out of varied experience. Certainly "the modern
consciousness," with which Jung has identified himself in
unmistakable places in his writing, "abhors" faith. But to
allow this abhorrence to affect statements which are presented
as strictly psychological will not do. Neither psychology
nor any other science is competent to investigate the truth of
the belief in God. It is the right of their representatives to
keep aloof; it is not, within their disciplines, their right to
make judgments about the belief in God as about something
which they know.

The psychological doctrine which deals with mysteries
without knowing the attitude of faith towards mystery is
the modern manifestation of Gnosis. Gnosis is not to be
understood as only a historical category, but as a universal
one. It—and not atheism, which annihilates God because it
must reject the hitherto existing images of God—is the real
antagonist of the reality of faith. Its modern manifestation
concerns me specifically not only because of its massive pre-

tensions, but also in particular because of its resumption of the Carpocratian motif. This motif, which it teaches as psychotherapy, is that of mystically deifying the instincts instead of hallowing them in faith. That we must see C. G. Jung in connection with this modern manifestation of Gnosis I have proved from his statements and can do so in addition far more abundantly. His little "Abraxas" opus, which every unprejudiced reader will take to be not a poem as he says, but a confession, I have mentioned because here there is already proclaimed in all clarity the ambivalent Gnostic "God" who balances good and evil in Himself.

Notes to
"Religion and Modern Thinking"

CHAPTER V

1   *L'existentialisme est un humanisme* (1946), 21. All the quotations in this essay except one (see note 54) are translated directly and literally from the French or German original. For the context in translation cf. *Existentialism*, translated by Bernard Frechtman (1947), 18.

2   *Situations* I (1947), 153, Section "*Un nouveau mystique*" of 1943.

3   *L'existentialisme*, 33 f. Cf. *Existentialism*, 27 f.

4   *Situations* I, *loc. cit.*

5   Isaiah 45:15.

6   *Situations* I, *loc. cit.*

7   *Ibid.*, 154.

8   *L'existentialisme*, 93. Cf. *Existentialism*, 60.

9   *Situations* I, 237, Section "*Aller et retour*," probably of 1942.

10   *L'être et le néant* (1943), Section "*L'existence d'autrui.*"

11   *Situations* I, *loc. cit.*

12   *Situations* I, 334, Section "*La liberté cartésienne.*"

13   *L'être et le néant*, 286 f., 341.

14   *L'existentialisme*, 33 ff. Cf. *Existentialism*, 25 ff.

15   *Ibid.*, 47. Cf. *Existentialism*, 33.

16   *Ibid.*, 36. Cf. *Existentialism*, 27.

17   *Ibid.*, 89. Cf. *Existentialism*, 58.

18   *Holzwege* (1950), 193 ff., Section "*Nietzsches Wort 'Gott ist tot.'*"

19   *Vom Wesen des Grundes* (1929), 28.

20   *Platons Lehre von der Wahrheit. Mit einem Brief über den Humanismus* (1947), 102 f.

21   *Ibid.*, 75.

22 *Ibid.,* 85 f.

23 *Erläuterungen zu Hölderlins Dichtungen* (1944), 2nd Ed. (1951), 44, Section "*Hölderlin und das Wesen der Dichtung*" of 1936. For an English translation of "*Hölderlin und das Wesen der Dichtung*" cf. Martin Heidegger, *Existence and Being* (1949), "*Hölderlin and the Essence of Poetry.*"

24 *Ibid.,* 26.

25 *Ibid.,* 27.

26 *Ibid.,* 108, Section "*Andenken*" of 1943.

27 *Platons Lehre,* 76.

28 *Erläuterungen,* 66, Section "*Wie wenn am Feiertage*" of 1941.

29 *Erläuterungen,* 37.

30 *Die Selbstbehauptung der deutschen Universität,* 22.

31 *Freiburger Studentenzeitung* of Nov. 3, 1933.

32 *Erläuterungen,* 73.

33 It should be noticed that the term "thought" ("*das Denken*") in the late writings of Heidegger is used in essence to describe his own thought.

34 *Psychologie und Religion* (1942), 133. This passage is not in the English edition.

35 Wilhelm-Jung, *Das Geheimnis der goldenen Blüte* (1929), 73. Cf. Wilhelm-Jung, *The Secret of the Golden Flower,* translated by Cary F. Baynes (1935), 135.

36 Jung-Kerényi, *Einführung in das Wesen der Mythologie* (1941), 109. Cf. C. G. Jung and K. Kerényi, *Essays on a Science of Mythology* (1949), 102.

37 *Die Beziehungen zwischen dem Ich und dem Unbewussten* (1928), 205. Cf. *Two Essays on Analytical Psychology,* translated by H. G. and C. F. Baynes (1928), "The Relation between the Ego and the Unconscious," 267.

38 *Psychologische Typen* (1921), 340. Cf. *Psychological Types,* translated by H. G. Baynes (1923), 300 f.

39 *Geheimnis,* 73. Cf. *The Secret of the Golden Flower,* 135.

40 *Typen*, 340. Cf. *Psychological Types*, 300.

41 *Geheimnis*, 73. Cf. *The Secret of the Golden Flower*, 135.

42 Evans-Wentz, *Das tibetanische Totenbuch "Bardo Thödol"* (1936), 18.

43 *Psychologie und Alchemie* (1944), 28. *Psychology and Alchemy*, translated by R. F. C. Hull (1952).

44 *Totenbuch*, 19.

45 There is no expression similar to this to be found in the philosophers of the preceding century who, like Fries and Beneke, wished to base metaphysics on psychology.

46 Cf. *"Der Geist der Psychologie"* (*Eranos-Jahrbuch*, 1946), 460 ff.

47 *Seelenprobleme der Gegenwart* (1931), 417. Cf. *Modern Man in Search of a Soul*, translated by W. F. Dell and C. F. Baynes (1933), 239.

48 *Geheimnis*, 73. Cf. *The Secret of the Golden Flower*, 135.

49 Cf. especially the second part of the sentence cited above from *"Seelenprobleme"* 417: "Modern consciousness . . . wishes to *know*, i.e., to have primal experience" with the sentence contained in the same book (p. 83): "We moderns are directed to experience again the spirit, i.e. to make primal experience." Cf. *Modern Man*, 140.

50 *Ibid.*, 327. Cf. *Modern Man*, 217 f.

51 *Ibid.*, 77. Cf. *Modern Man*, 135.

52 *Religion*, 145 ff. Cf. *Psychology and Religion*, 97 ff.

53 *Beziehungen*, 203 ff. Cf. *Two Essays on Analytical Psychology*, 267.

54 *The Integration of the Personality*, translated by S. M. Dell (1940), "The Development of Personality," 291 f. Cf. *Wirklichkeit der Seele* (1934), Lecture *"Vom Werden der Persönlichkeit"* of 1932, 197 f.

55 *Wirklichkeit der Seele*, 208 f. Cf. *The Integration of the Personality*, 302 f.

56 *Beziehungen*, 205. Cf. *Two Essays*, 267.

57 *Geheimnis,* 61. Cf. *The Secret,* 80.

58 Cf. *Religion,* 139 ff.; *Psychology and Religion,* 94 ff.

59 "*Der Geist der Psychologie,*" 477.

60 *Ibid.,* 474.

61 "Since God alone is free and uncreated, he is like the soul in being free—but not in uncreatedness, for the soul is created." Sermon 13, Raymond Blakney, *Meister Eckhart, A Modern Translation* (1941), 159. For original cf. *Predigten,* ed. Quint, 13 f.

62 "*Über das Selbst*" (*Eranos-Jahrbuch,* 1948), 315. Cf. *Psychologie und Alchemie,* 61.

63 *Symbolik des Geistes* (1948), 385.

64 *Ibid.,* 410.

65 "*Das Wandlungssymbol in der Messe*" (*Eranos-Jahrbuch,* 1940-1941), 153 f.

66 *Symbolik,* 439. Cf. *Religion,* 108 ff.; "*Zur Psychologie der Trinitätsidee*" (*Eranos-Jahrbuch,* 1940-1941), 51 ff.; *Alchemie,* 212.

67 *Symbolik,* 417.

68 *Alchemie,* 22 f.

69 *Religion* 172 f. Cf. *Psychology and Religion,* 106.

70 *Symbolik,* 409. Cf. "*Selbst,*" 304.

71 *Religion,* 111. Cf. *Psychology and Religion,* 74.

72 Cf. especially *Religion,* 175 f. (*Psychology and Religion,* 107 ff.)

73 *Holzwege,* 235. A comparison is to be recommended with Jung's expression "The interregnum is full of danger" in its context (*Psychologie und Religion,* 158), which means almost the opposite. (The passage is not in *Psychology and Religion,* which differs from the German edition.)

Index

Abraham, 6, 49, 52, 115-18
"Abraxas," 137
Absolute, the, 71, 96, 97 f., 119 f.,
  127; and the concrete, 41 f.; and
  moral absoluteness, 18, 97 ff.,
  100-107, 110 f., 115; and the
  particular, 41; and personality,
  28; and the universal, 40; apes
  of, 123 ff.; concept of, vs. love
  of, 50; made to appear unreal
  by philosophy, 123; objectified
  by philosophy, 31 f., 38-40, 124
Absolute Other, 67 f.
Absolute Personality, 60, 96 f.
Absurd, the, 116
Adam and Eve, 24
Aeschylus, 28 ff., 101
Agamemnon, 117
Agamemnon, 28
Anaximander, 100
Anonymous Jamblichi, 108
Anthropomorphism, 14-17
Antichrist, 89
"Art of Mistrust," 108
Artistic communication, 43
Asceticism, 38
Atheism, 71, 110, 136; critical, 46;
  existentialist, 65 f.; materialist,
  66
Augustine, 107

Being, 60, 70-74, 77
Bible, Hebrew, 33, 36 f., 42, 56 f.,
  90, 115-19
Biblical, *see* Bible, Hebrew
Book of Transformations, 100
Buddha, 27 f.
Buddhism, 96

Carpocratian motif, 137
Charisma, 78
Christ, 89 ff., 105
Christianity, 105 ff.
Christian conception of God, 90
  110; individualism, 106; peoples,
  106; symbolic, 89; tradition, 118
Class struggle, 109
Cogito, 39, 74
Cohen, Hermann, 53-62
Collective unconscious, 65, 82, 85,
  88; *see also* Unconscious, the
Coming One, the, 74, 76 f., 91
Confucius, 37, 100
Conscience, 86 f., 120
Consciousness, 39 f., 71, 126; mod-
  ern, 83 f., 86, 136; *see also* Sub-
  jectivity
Covenant of absolute with con-
  crete, 41; of Israel with God,
  103, 105 f.
Cratylus, 29

Dante and Beatrice, 59
Deification of instincts, 136; of
  man, 86, 90 ff.
Demonic God penetrates, 21;
  temptation, 118
Descartes, 19, 39 f.
Dialogue between God and Man,
  17, 75 f., 105, 107, 124 ff.; *see
  also* God, encounter with, liv-
  ing relation with; I-Thou rela-
  tion; Reciprocity, 99 f.
Dike, 99 f.
Divine attributes, 15 f., 100
Divine right of kings, 107
Duty, 115